THANKS FOR STOPPING BY

TALES OF LOVE AND LOSS FROM THE WORLD'S
GREATEST SENIOR DOG SANCTUARY

PENNY MILLER

Thanks for Stopping By – Tales of Love and Loss from the World's Greatest Senior Dog Sanctuary
Copyright © 2023 by Penny Miller / The Ministry of Dog Publishing

All rights reserved. No part of this book may be reproduced or transmitted in any form or by any means without written permission from the author.

ISBN 979-8-9853412-8-7 (soft cover)
ISBN 979-8-9853412-9-4 (eBook)

Other titles by Penny Miller:

Cut the Crap – A Simple No Nonsense Guide To Feeding Your Dog
Frosty-Faced and F*cking Fabulous! - Love, Life & Good Health with your Senior Dog
It's OK He's Friendly – The Canine Behavior Guide Your Dog Wants You To Read
Ouch! – A Simple Guide to Pain and Inflammation in your Dog

Available at www.theministryofdog.com

COVER PHOTOGRAPH

This beautiful photograph sums up our mission.

Here is the incredible Adele, who came to us in August 2021 and left us in December 2021.

A short stay for sure, but oh, so powerful and oh, so poignant.

In this beautiful photograph you see her giving her unique gifts of time, love and kindness to this sweet lady on one of our community visits.

Adele came to us aged 13, her small body wracked with issues. Horribly aggressive and untreatable mammary tumors that threatened to take her at any moment, a serious heart condition including heartworms, as well as dental disease, but none of these stopped her from smiling.

Adele never concentrated on her heavy burdens, she concentrated only on the gifts she carried.

She would insist on going on every community visit as if she knew her days were numbered and planned to cram as much in to each hour, each minute, each second, as she possibly could.

Together with her foster mum, Cindy Vaughn, they were an unbeatable team spreading joy and love to those needing it, and they opened up avenues of communication and emotional sharing every time.

How do you change the world?

Just like this.

ACKNOWLEDGEMENTS

To our incredible team of volunteers without whom there would be no Frankie and Andy's Place Senior Dog Sanctuary, thank you to all of you from the very core of my being for everything you do. Especially thank you for the time you give and the selfless way you love and care for our seniors. You are number one in these acknowledgements because you are number one in our mission.

To the rescues and shelters that we partner with year in, year out, thank you so much for the work that you do saving dogs from death row. God bless you, all of you. It is our great privilege to work both with you and beside you.

To our wonderful team of cabin staff, led by Jen Calderhead, who go above and beyond every day to care for these special souls and who make it look easy, when it really isn't, our deepest thanks.

To my wonderful husband, partner, best friend and all-round top fella, Peter, who partners with me in everything I do, and who calmly helps to make it happen but adamantly refuses recognition or fuss. He lives by the creed "It's all about the dogs, and only about the dogs". Without him, there would be no Frankie and Andy's Place. Thank you, sweetheart.

To my sons Jake and Joe who never once said "Can you please just stop rescuing dogs?" and who were happy to do whatever it took to save a life, or improve a life, thank you.

To Kristen Snyder, Ranch manager, thank you for all of the sleepless nights, the OCD you have about our residents, the double and triple checking, the following round behind, and the frequent McDonalds runs in the middle of the night to get dogs to eat.

To Angelita Green, Dr Ellen Steinberg and Cliff Jolliff, thank you so very much for all that you contribute to Frankie and Andy's Place, every day of every year. We are beyond blessed to have you on our board.

To our own personal dogs, every single one a rescue, every single one an exceptional teacher; Nelson, Simba, Freddie, Noodle, Steve Miller, Levi, Ava, Colin, Hoss and Snazzy, thank you all of you.

Penny and Krystle Andrews, who understood our dream of a senior dog sanctuary, and vowed they'd help us to make it happen. These two ladies made the most selfless contribution of all time in helping us to get this mission off the ground in 2015, and still continue to provide support every day. Every day we thank our lucky stars that we met the 'Andrews Sisters'.

A huge thank you to our donors and supporters who have given so generously to our mission and helped us to provide a beautiful forever home to so many end of life dogs who never dreamed they'd get this lucky! A simple 'Thank you' never seems quite enough, but we always hope that the smiling and relaxed faces you have helped us to create give you peace of mind, happiness and a solid return on your investment.

Finally, a huge thankyou to Dr. Don Baker and his wife, Judy. These two individuals are almost wholly responsible for the timing of my eulogies. You see, without them, and their simply incredible, life-saving and life changing product, Dr Baker's Canine System Saver, most of our dogs would have passed a lot, lot sooner than they did.

CONTENTS

Who Are We And What Do We Do?	1
About the Author	7
Introduction	9
🐾 A letter from Isaac Hayes to his owner	11
🐾 Farewell to Colin, the very first Frankie and Andy's Place dog	16
🐾 Farewell to Donald O'Connor, our luscious, low-riding pelvis pusher	27
🐾 Farewell to Tallulah Bankhead, our very own sunshine girl	33
🐾 Farewell to Holly Hunter, she came, she saw, she kicked plenty of ass	39
🐾 Farewell to Kiefer Sutherland 'He ain't heavy, he's my brother'	43
🐾 Farewell to Grace our very own 'Amazing Grace'	47
🐾 Farewell to Frannie the wonder dog, who stole our hearts	52
🐾 Farewell to Yogi Berra, the special boy who launched a movement	56
🐾 Farewell to Olivia Newton John, a bundle of love and joy in a dog's body	61

- 🐾 Farewell to David Beckham, who had us at 'Hello' — 67
- 🐾 Welcome to Meemaw, for as long as we can enjoy you — 72
- 🐾 Farewell to MeeMaw, an angel who came down to earth, and ended up staying a while — 74
- 🐾 Farewell to Lily Tomlin, the funny girl who tried to shank us all… — 78
- 🐾 Farewell to Snazzy, who lived, laughed and loved…fiercely — 82
- 🐾 Farewell to Iain Glen, our amber-eyed heart-throb — 90
- 🐾 Farewell to Parker Posey, our perfect, snowy enchantress — 95
- 🐾 Farewell to Orville Redenbacher, who stole our hearts with his goodbye — 98
- 🐾 Farewell to Trisha Yearwood, our beautiful golden child — 104
- 🐾 Farewell to Bill Murray, such a sweet and gentle soul — 107
- 🐾 Farewell to Patti Labelle, the happiest dog in the world — 111
- 🐾 Farewell to Meryl Streep, a ballsier broad we never knew… — 115
- 🐾 Farewell to Lil Kim, First lady of Frankie and Andy's Place — 121
- 🐾 Farewell to Boris Karloff, First Gentleman of Frankie and Andy's Place — 126
- 🐾 Farewell to Frankie, Godfather of the mission, and the one who started it all… — 134

WHO ARE WE AND WHAT DO WE DO?

Frankie and Andy's Place is a unique combination of a 'final chapter' home for very old dogs, a hospice sanctuary for dogs of any age, and an emotional healing center for troubled humans.

We have three beautifully appointed log cabins, that are really just like small human homes, nestled in a picturesque three acre Barrow County woodland setting, with each cabin dedicated to size and temperament of dogs.

We have a 'Littles cabin' for dogs up to 20 pounds, a 'Bigs cabin' for dogs over 20 pounds and then another cabin that works for anything in between and provides a solution for the overflow from either cabin. We also have a small number of dogs in individual foster homes.

The cabins are luxuriously appointed, complete with rugs, leather couches and chairs for both the humans who visit and the dogs who prefer a little height to relax on...as well as soft, soft dog beds. There is a whirlpool bath, a full kitchen and we have a wonderful sunporch in each cabin for residents to relax on loungers and beds while enjoying the breeze. Each cabin has its' own yard but all cabin residents are walked regularly, weather and achy bones permitting, on the woodland walking trails at the rear of the property.

Our mission centers around providing holistic care...so first and foremost a stress free environment, food that is freshly cooked each day and tailored to each dog's individual needs, and plenty of sunshine, fresh air and the company of good friends as well as their new 'family', the wonderful volunteers and staff. We use an integrative approach, with a mix of mainly expert veterinary care combined with the judicious use of some alternative therapies.

Frankie and Andy's Place is home to 30 or so (the number is constantly changing) gentle, loving, senior dogs who have been cruelly cast aside by their humans and yet who still have many valuable gifts to share. These dogs are then 'repurposed' as therapy dogs to go out into the community where they share gifts of sympathy, time, reassurance and unconditional love with the humans who need them. These may be folks in elder facilities no longer able to have dogs of their own, or special needs children in classrooms or the differently-abled in a local Adult Daycare Center.

We have found that if a dog has a job where his unique gifts are appreciated, he feels he has value. If he feels valued, he will blossom and thrive and then he can pass on his joy to the community, which all of our dogs do, every week.

THANKS FOR STOPPING BY

Our dogs have touched the lives of thousands of people in our short 8 years of operation and in 2024, our community outreach will be expanding to include even more children in schools and others who need us locally. Every day, we provide a serene and comfortable experience for the dogs to work their magic at the cabins, where our 40 plus volunteers each come once a week to help look after the dogs, and in so doing, find their own solace and contentment.

It has long been our motto that in looking after others, we focus less on our own issues. Less focus means they tend to shrink.

At the cabins, friendships are forged, problems are forgotten and the dogs provide the therapy that is much needed. Most of our volunteers have been with us for six plus years, all of them seeing the cabins as their second home, all of them committed to giving these dogs what they need in their last days, and to be with them until they draw their final breath.

We bring our dogs in from licensed rescues and shelters only; we do not take owner surrenders at all, and this is because part of our mission is to help 'clear the backlog' of unadoptable dogs that so frequently stops rescues from being able to take in the neglect or abuse cases that they find locally. We work hand in hand with around 25 rescues and shelters in Georgia, Tennessee, Alabama and the Carolinas, enabling them to free up space in their own facilities and foster programs and continue to do the work they do, without being spatially or financially challenged by the chronically ill cases that they try to help and often get stuck with.

In 2022, we set up an advice and resource service called 'Senior Solutions @ Frankie and Andy's Place' for those who are in crisis and would seek to rehome their dogs. For these people we offer free behavioral advice, links to helpful resources and help with food etc in an attempt to keep dogs with their families where possible. Last year we helped many families find alternative solutions to rehoming their pets. We have also helped to rehome a number of dogs where death, chronic illness or homelessness have been the issues.

In the summer of 2023, we launched our "Helping hands, Healing Paws' outreach mission. This is an extension to our existing outreach activities; here we take dog food, cat food, much needed items and human comfort essentials out onto the streets in local cities, to help the homeless population. We also provide dog food and other items to folks who cannot afford to feed their animals, and we also give food, supplements and necessary items to other rescues and shelters. We have a large container on site at the facility for storage and a mobile trailer for taking these items out to where they are needed.

We have always lived by the saying "be the change you wish to see in the world" and, while we are not perfect, we figure that if we keep reaching out, keep learning, keep finding ways to do more and give more, we can change the world.

If not for everyone, at least for some.

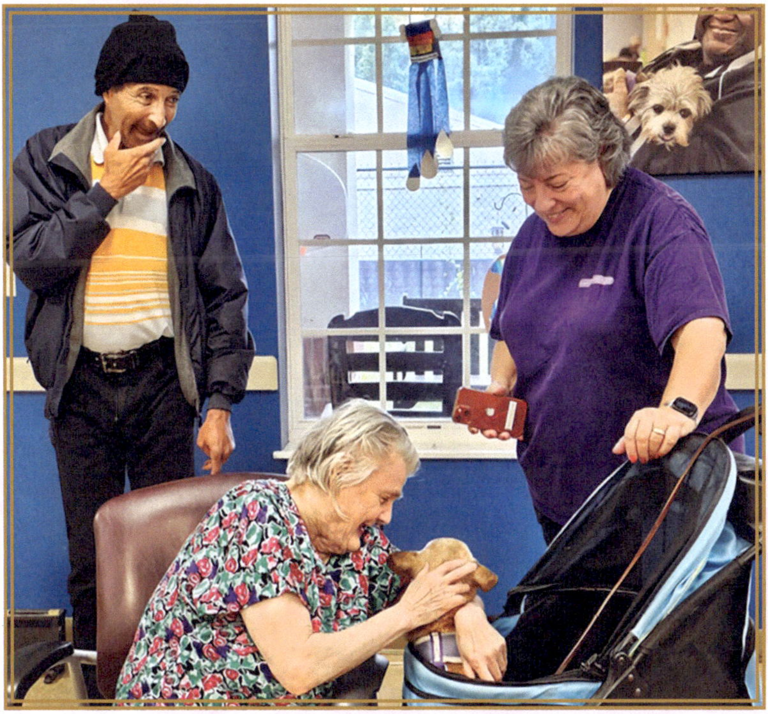

THANKS FOR STOPPING BY

PENNY MILLER

ABOUT THE AUTHOR

Penny Miller is a British-born Canine Behaviour Counsellor, based in Georgia, USA.

In 2006, she and her husband Peter created the award winning holistic canine boarding and rehabilitation Ranch, Desperate Dogs, where fun, freedom, kindness, great food and a one on one approach to training and rehabilitation are key to their thousands of success stories.

In 2015, along with Peter and friends Penny and Krystle Andrews, they founded Frankie and Andy's Place Senior Dog

Sanctuary, a beautiful end of life and hospice facility for cast aside senior dogs as well as an emotional healing center for humans.

She was a co-founder of 'Off the Chain USA', a charity that provides fencing and dog houses to chained dogs.

A prolific writer, this is her fifth published book; she also writes a regular blog called "The Dog's Honest Truth" and in addition runs a nationwide advice service, 'Senior Solutions' at Frankie and Andy's Place, a resource for dog owners in need to help reduce needless euthanasia and limit owner surrender numbers.

Penny spends what's left of her day studying to become a licensed veterinary naturopath.

INTRODUCTION

A eulogy is, in many ways, a love letter to the deceased.

It is a way to praise and honor them, to show our respect not only for their life but for the contribution they have made to ours.

When I write eulogies for, or stories about, the dogs at Frankie and Andy's Place, there is a further element, though...

It is to show that they were loved.

It is to show that they were 'seen'.

It is to show that they mattered.

The dogs that come to us at Frankie and Andy's Place Senior Dog Sanctuary arrive with nothing but broken dreams, broken bodies and broken hearts.

Given up by their former families in their last days, right when they need the security of them the most, some of our seniors are emotionally lost, asking themselves what they did wrong? Others are hideously neglected to varying degrees, some are horrifically abused, but all have one thing in common...they are simply looking for love.

For the time that they are with us, no matter whether it is three days or three years, we strive to repair their bodies, mend their hearts and fulfil their dreams.

From the moment they arrive, we embark on a journey of discovery, joyously uncovering and celebrating their unique personalities, 'roll on the floor' laughing at their various peccadilloes and always, always seeing the beauty within their souls.

Dogs are not one dimensional creatures, they have a myriad of emotions, a cornucopia of talents and a vast array of personality traits that delight, shock, annoy and amuse.

Just like humans.

These eulogies seek to tell their stories and to shine a light on them as individuals, lest we ever forget that they were here, they had stories to tell and that they had so much to contribute.

At time of writing, we have saved 140 souls.

140 special creatures who, through their very existence, have created a village of carers who became good friends, family even…both for the dogs, and for each other.

140 creatures who have taught us all so many things we never knew…about dogs, and even about ourselves.

140 abandoned souls, who, in their relief and gratitude finding themselves with us, gave us more reasons to live, love and laugh than we ever knew existed.

This book is a celebration of life as much as it is a frequently hilarious peek at the inner workings of our miraculous, award-winning senior dog sanctuary.

A place where dogs have the time of their lives, for the last times of their lives.

A special place that they leave knowing they were loved, they were seen, and oh, how they mattered!

A LETTER FROM ISAAC HAYES TO HIS OWNER

MARCH 2022

Dear Daddy,

There are some things I have to tell you.

Daddy, that day a couple of weeks ago that you dropped me off at Walton County Animal Control was the worst day of my life. Your walking in with me the way you did, totally perplexed the intake receptionist. She was very surprised that you just said "I want to surrender my dog because we don't have time to look after him any more".

I couldn't at first understand what you were saying to her because all I could hear were the dogs crying and screaming in the pens out back...

"I want my family!"

"When are my people coming back for me?"

"Where did my neighbor in the pen next door go to? Why didn't they bring him back?"

"Did I do something wrong to make them dump me? I tried to be a good dog and protect them all my life, so why am I here?"

It was so, so awful to hear...

Listening to their frantic cries made me sad but I felt safe because I was with you Daddy, right by your side, like always.

That is, until you left me there to be just like them; forgotten, unwanted, scared and with a broken heart.

Remember when you got me, Daddy? You brought me into the family home 15 years ago, and you were so excited because I was cute and small and you promised there and then to love me forever, didn't you?

And now, here I am, a confused old dog, with creaky bones and feeling in a little bit of pain.

Now, right when I need you the most, you don't love me anymore.

You have time to watch football, to go to the mall and to look at your phone for hours on end, but you tell that lady you don't have time enough to look after me?

I don't even ask for much, Daddy.

Is it because I get confused? I'm sorry Daddy, I can't help it... but you know I don't ever cause any mischief, I just pace a little.

Is it because I needed a soft bed for my old bones? They don't cost much, Daddy, and I would have been just as happy with an old blanket if it meant staying with the family I have known so long. Because you see, you are my family, and I know you, and that familiarity is important to me as I get old.

I was so scared in that shelter, although the people were very kind, I just paced and paced, waiting for you to come back. I didn't even eat because I knew there would be food in my own bowl waiting for me when you came to take me home.

Days and days I waited, knowing it had all been a huge mistake, sure that this was all a bad dream.

But yet, you never came.

And then a lady called Cindy came to meet me. She gently took me out of my cage and looked me all over, she had me meet a few other dogs and then she talked to another lady far away on the phone and they were both saying 'yes'.

Then I heard these words, "We will give this boy a forever home, he can come with us, we have a perfect spot for him". The shelter lady was smiling so happily, and all of a sudden Cindy was helping me into her car.

She brought me to a very kind couple called Bill and Kathie, who took me into their home and cared for me for five days while I relaxed a little and had a chance to catch my breath. The shelter had been so noisy you see, all of the dogs just pace morning and night, so it was hard for me to sleep there.

They were so kind and so patient with me, they even held me when I cried for you, Daddy.

Then, one beautiful Spring day, I was brought to Frankie and Andy's Place. It's a bunch of beautiful cabins in the woods where birds sing, butterflies dance on the breeze and everyone's heart is full of love.

It's simply perfect here, Daddy.

There are so many people who take care of me, volunteers who love on me and staff who create wonderful fresh food and arrange soft sleeping places. They pet me and brush me, massage me and tell me all the time that I matter, that I am beautiful. They even put me in a snazzy new warm coat of my very own.

Yes, I do feel kind of special here.

All the other dogs that live here (there are 30 of them!) are very old, and some are even dying, but they are all happy and very relaxed. They are very gentle and kind and they tell me that I do not have to worry ever again, that this is my forever home. They tell me that this huge new human family will love me all the rest of my days and that I will never again be apart from them.

I believe them.

I am slowly feeling the fear and panic leave my heart and I am learning to trust again. It is like a huge weight is being lifted from my frail, old body.

But Daddy, you must know that you are one day going to be old like me?

You will rely on your family to be there for you just like I did, and I truly hope that they are.

I hope that no-one ever does to you what you did to me.

For you see, there is nothing worse in the world than to love unconditionally and to be not loved that way in return.

And Daddy, even though you did not care enough for me, and were prepared to just leave me at that shelter knowing that I would likely die that day because of my old body and the fact that it is so overcrowded, I would never, no, not ever, wish that on you.

Because, you see, I am a dog.

I am perfect and pure of heart.

When I commit to you, it is forever and so I will still continue to love you always, no matter what you did to me.

Everyone here gets a new name when they arrive. It is so they can throw off the shackles of their old life in their beautiful new home with their new family. Calling us by our old names can invoke difficult memories, they say, and they just want us to be happy.

My new name, thanks to the kindly lady, Kathie, who fostered me, is Isaac Hayes. The name Isaac means 'one who rejoices, one who laughs'.

THANKS FOR STOPPING BY

I know that I am rejoicing at my good fortune and that I will laugh again.

Everywhere I go here, they are saying "Welcome to your new home Isaac, you are loved".

This time, Daddy, I can trust that it is forever.

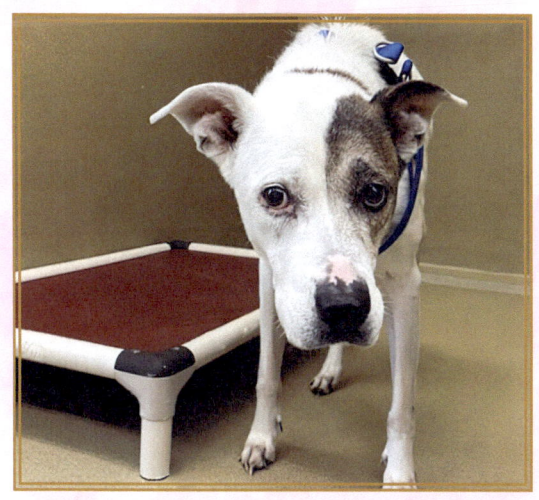

FAREWELL TO COLIN, THE VERY FIRST FRANKIE AND ANDY'S PLACE DOG

APRIL 2017

>Do not go gentle into that good night...
>Old age should burn and rave at close of day
>Rage, rage against the dying of the light...
>**(Dylan Thomas)**

Yesterday we lost our dear boy Colin. It was so, so hard but it was the right thing to do.

Was his body ready to go?

Yes.

He was in pain, this pain was causing unbelievable anxiety, and his legs gave out on him at every turn.

Did it sit comfortably with his head that his body had so failed him and that he must leave behind all that he had come to hold so dear?

No. No, it didn't.

For you see, Colin had a roller coaster life of great highs and huge lows...he has known absolute love...and abject misery. He has been adored...and he has been dumped, always by those he had placed his trust in...people who had committed to him, and then changed their mind when it no longer suited them to care for him.

But in the last almost two years, Colin found a permanent home where everything he did was okay.

"Your legs gave out on you old friend? Never mind, we'll just scoop you back up and set you on your way again."

"Pooped on the carpet? No biggie, mate, we will take care of that."

"Peed on the floor? Well, how great is that? I get the chance to try out that new turbo mop!"

'Terrified of thunder storms and having an anxiety attack?..... well, we will stay with you until the storm is over.'

Shouldn't every senior dog, every dog in the world even, have that level of understanding? Sadly this is so often not the case.

I first met Colin when I was the on call behaviorist for Gracie's Place Pet Rescue, in 2009. Joni who ran the rescue had pulled this dashing adult male Pointer / American Bulldog mix from Elburton Animal Shelter where he had been sitting desperately waiting for anyone to come to his aid for weeks. She took a shine to him despite being told by the vet who checked him out that he was aggressive and that she should have him euthanized. The shelter he had been in was cold and dark, he had a heavy load of heartworms, and he was pitiful. She was advised against taking him, but saw something in him that she immediately trusted. How wonderful for us all that she did, for this 'aggressive dog' turned out to be the pearl in the oyster at Gracie's Place. So gentle, slow and deliberate with a showstopping patience, this boy got a lot of interest from the get-go.

After getting him treated for heartworms, he was adopted out to a family locally who were warned that he was severely thunder phobic and could not, under any circumstances, be left alone in a storm. "We love dogs, this boy is going to be a part of our family, so he won't be left alone in thunderstorms, ever... promise!" They insisted.

Yes, promises, promises.

A few weeks later, we had the very worst storms imaginable and the bloody stupid owners left him in their garage while they went to get their nails done. Poor Colin was so panicked he tried to dig his way out of the garage door, severing his arteries in the process, and then, when that escape route didn't work, he smashed through the window and ran out into the street, collapsing on the neighbor's lawn. I can't even begin to imagine what Colin went through on that day, all I know is that he was terrified and felt alone and in pain. I can't bear that for anyone...

The neighbor thankfully saw him before he bled out, checked his tags, and called the rescue, who rushed to get him and immediately rescinded his adoption..

As part of his convalescence, he needed to have minimal exercise and so, despite me having told Joni that I would not foster for the rescue as I ran a boarding facility, I offered to take him in...just for the week, mind you, just the week! Mmmhhmmm!

Well, as per usual, that week turned into a month, then that month turned into ten, and it seemed that despite every offer, and multiple home visits, no one was really good enough to have Colin. He made himself useful, became the temporary concierge dog for the Desperate Dogs Ranch and taught us all about what dogs REALLY need to know, feel and do during a thunder storm.

Thanks to Colin, we now have a completely different level of expertise in dealing with this terrible problem, and we have been able to go on to help hundreds of dogs with serious issues thanks to his teaching.

If we have helped any of you reading this with your thunder phobic dog, you owe this old boy a great deal.

He spent his days, once he was well, working with me out on the land and then at night he would take care of our guest dogs... and watch the film 'Love actually' DVD on a continual loop. I swear that dog had a secret crush on Emma Thompson, his tail would wag every time she appeared during the film. We tried other movies, like Mission Impossible and Toy Story but he told us he wasn't an action movie kind of a guy...

Then, one day, a lady I knew told me she was looking for a seeing eye dog for her dog, Wrigley, who was almost blind. She had two lovely young daughters whom Colin adored instantly, and, after a trial run, during which he very naturally took on the role of caretaker for Wrigley, Colin was adopted. They loved him, he was such a clever boy and it was going to be happy ever after for him, wasn't it?

Wasn't it?

Over the next three or four years, this lady must have asked me four times if I would think about taking Colin back, because she was going to get divorced (of course she was keeping her other dog) or because he dug out of the yard (hmmm...put a concrete strip under the gate maybe???) or later it was because he was 'on his own so much after Wrigley died' (ummm...spend more time with him?).

There always seemed to be a reason he needed to go, despite her having committed to him, and despite how much her kids loved him.

I started to hate her for that, I must confess, because to us, a promise is a promise and a commitment is a commitment. This dear dog deserved love forever.

We couldn't take him in at that time as we had too little room, we were by then fostering other dogs of course, so I talked to her a lot about commitment, and the lessons we show our kids by our actions.

My husband Peter and I have endured many, many crises over the years but it has never occurred to us that life would be easier or better if we got rid of one of our dogs. To us, when you adopt, you adopt for life, and they become your children.

Trust me, my human kids have been much closer to being given away on occasion than any of our dogs.

I had him come visit us at the Ranch every now and then when I could, to give him fun and company, and to let him know he was still family and valued, but then one day in August 2015 she texted me to tell me that she was having him euthanized that morning.

He had fallen, couldn't get up and had 'lost the use of his legs'.

So I raced over to the vets determined to say goodbye, frightened of the pitiful sight that surely awaited me, and who do you think was walking unaided in through the doors of the vets? Who do you think broke free of his leash and raced (well, more like ambled, but in his mind he was jogging) over to see me, jumped up and licked my face?

Yup, you guessed it!

I didn't tell her what I thought of her, but instead took him home with me that day, despite us having literally just moved into new premises with the boarding facility and having so much to do and so much chaos, and honestly, so little money, but where else was he going to go?

Clearly this woman was looking for any excuse to get him gone, enough that she lied about his health. I came home to Pete with Colin in the back of the car, his head poking out of the window smiling ear to ear, it was quite the turnaround.

While my beloved husband was as always overjoyed to see this boy, he was a bit shocked to see him alive and in my car after his planned euthanasia.

"Ummm, where's he going to sleep, then? It's not like we have a lot of room is it?" He asked me, one eyebrow wriggling like Roger Moore, as he tried to keep a straight face.

"Look" I said, "We have always talked about starting a senior dog sanctuary haven't we? I mean, I know it wasn't going to be yet, but sometimes God has other plans. Colin is old and he needs a home, so we can keep him just 'til the sanctuary is up and running and he could go live up there, right? He'll be our first dog!"

Pete, as he always does, just shook his head, laughed, and said "Okay, I guess we got ourselves our very first senior sanctuary resident then. I better start thinking of how we are going to get this thing built because we don't have room for you to do this again!"

True to his word, he embarked on his mission with zest and started raising funds to get our senior sanctuary built, which we did, nine months later.

Colin quickly embraced life at the Ranch, back again among his old pals from our working pack Levi and Ava, Freddie, Snazzy and Hoss. He discovered a new purpose in taking care of the little dogs, along with his 'mini me' friend Snazzy, and the two of them let all the tinies jump all over them, run rings around them and lick their ears. I'd be walking in the field with the 'Bigs' and he'd be in the smaller yard with some 5 pound terrorists, letting them jump all over his head and use him as a roundabout, all the while looking at me smiling as if to say "This is the absolute BEST, Mama!!!"

After the sanctuary was built in April 2016, and we started to fill it with dogs, we would often think that it was time Colin 'move house' and go live in the senior dog sanctuary that was his planned home. We tried him up there a couple of times, but the truth was, he loved his family down at the boarding ranch so much, he cried when he was away from them and we felt he had already had so much loss and misery in his life, could we put him through more?

Of course not, so Colin became the very first Senior Sanctuary dog who never spent more than one night up at the Sanctuary. We convinced ourselves that this was a better course of action, so that we would have space to give another needy dog up at the sanctuary if he stayed down with us.

Win/win.

Slow, ambling and a true 'Steady Eddie' Colin never did anything with any pressing urgency, unless of course he saw the UPS guy pull up in the driveway, and then the stubborn old bulldog in him would come racing to the fore. He'd tear up the field to tell him to 'bugger off' and get out of his driveway full of piss and vinegar.

"Oh and that box you're delivering? Well, it BETTER be treats from Chewy!!!"

Trouble was, he then had to get all the way back to the house from the field, which always took him ten times longer than it did to get out there, after all that effort.

Colin was like something out of an Old Western, I always imagined him to talk like John Wayne when he used to say "Why I oughta…" and put his fists up ready to start a fight, full of bluster.

But then again, he walked like Robert Mitchum….stiff and determined with a bit of a 'Big Man Swagger'. Of course, he couldn't back it up, he was so much weaker by then, but in his mind he was Clint Eastwood, and we never, ever burst his bubble.

Just before Thanksgiving in 2016 he had a stroke, stopped eating, couldn't move and we honestly thought it was his time.

We made plans to say goodbye and I had a chat with him as we got him ready for the ride to the vet. I told him if this was his time, he was for sure letting us know in no uncertain terms.

However, if it wasn't his time, then he had better get his ass up and start eating quickly, or at least look a bit lively and show us a spark of something, anything.

Sure enough, he rallied around within thirty minutes and so his trip to the vets was swiftly changed and ended up with him getting a steroid shot, something we did regularly in the months that followed, just to keep him mobile. It worked to give him quality of life and maintain his dignity, something that was everything to him.

Two months ago, we noticed he was starting to look a little skeletal, the muscle atrophy on his head was plain to see. He was still happy but we paid very close attention.

Then a month ago, his eyes sank into his head somewhat. He was in pain but it was almost manageable, and he still had some quality of life, playing and wrestling softly on the carpet with his pack brother Hoss every day, eating up a storm and barking at anyone he felt like.

A week ago, the play stopped and it seems he was just going through the motions; painful, haunted looking and with such advanced knuckling that his skin scraped off his inner toes as he walked. He collapsed every few yards, and we painstakingly helped him back up and on his way but we knew then it was just a matter of time. We tried everything in our power, but nothing was fixing it this time.

On Monday he told me it was time. I gave him 24 hours to think about it, to see if he would bounce back like he had so many times before.

Yesterday morning he said "Yes, this is it Mama. I can't be in this body anymore, it hurts too much. I really don't want to leave but I have no choice".

We arranged for the vet to come to the house at 4pm, and I took him out to the park at Fort Yargo and for lunch before she came. I wanted his last day to be special with McDonalds burgers, a beautiful view, a time of serenity as we talked about what he could expect, what heaven would be like, the whole nine yards.

I'd love to say that this was the romantic ending that so many of our dogs are lucky enough to have, but in all honesty it wasn't.

He panicked during the car ride because he knew that it was time, that despite his body being past due for it, his mind was not and he didn't want it. During our very brief walk at Fort Yargo, he read my mind and knew what was coming I am certain, and so he tried to run away from me, despite the fact his legs would not work and he was collapsing every few feet.

Back at the Ranch, he kept trying to get back to the office where he had his sofa bed as we led him to the field, our plan being that he could rest on a blanket with his friends nearby and breathe in the sunshine as he passed...and yet we felt like we were leading him to the gallows.

Logic says there was no choice. His body was done. He could not take any more pain and the stress of not coping with his pain was killing him. It was strangling him, from the inside out.

We couldn't bear to watch it happen and yet we knew that to allow it to go on was the worst kind of hateful act.

Colin passed away with his head on my lap, on a blanket under the Dogwood tree, flanked by our working pack. Levi was sitting right beside him, Ava was watching everything from a respectful distance and Hoss came and kissed his friend goodbye, as did Freddie.

They knew, they all knew...I wish I had their intelligence, they see a much bigger picture than we do.

PENNY MILLER

Today, we console ourselves with the good stuff...the fact that he never heard a cross word, was absolutely assured of our love for him every day that we knew him, and that we kept our promise.

Our promise was to love him unconditionally, to let him tell us when he was ready, that we would preserve his dignity and that we would always, always take the best possible care of him.

It is all we can do for those we love, isn't it?

FAREWELL TO DONALD O'CONNOR, OUR LUSCIOUS, LOW-RIDING PELVIS PUSHER

JANUARY 2017

Donald, Donald, Donald…

Sex God, Treat Whore, Bedhog, Disco Diva, Mexican Jumping Bean and Falsetto Crooner……all things to all dog lovers, this spunky lil' low rider trotted into our lives in June 2016, with his Robert Redford good looks and his humongous personality.

I had been sent a listing on him by one of our rescue friends who told me that he had a maximum two days before he was being put to sleep. Apparently he was unadoptable due to his health issues.

He was in Cobb County Animal Shelter, but we just couldn't get to him in time, so we called on our friends at Dream Dachshund Rescue to go take a look at him for us, to see if he would be a fit. If he was, then we would call and put a hold on him.

Well...Dream volunteer Vikki went to the shelter on a Sunday afternoon, the day before he was scheduled for euthanasia and quickly grabbed him. She told me later that no way was she leaving that darling dog there, even if we couldn't take him... he was so bloody handsome and so bloody cheeky looking, that she just could not drive away without him. So she scooped him up, popped him on the front seat of her car, and drove home to Atlanta all the way with her windows open....because his fetid breath was so disgusting.

Bad heart murmur, upper respiratory infection, tumors that were squashing his internal organs, teeth that were so bad they were killing him slowly with the bacteria, a 'chesticle' tumor that hung down beneath his chest and scraped the ground as he walked...it looked like his 'junk' had been stuck in the wrong place...

Nothing should have worked on this old guy, and yet everything that mattered, did.

At 16 years of age, he had clearly had a rough life with little care of note, but he still approached life like a wide eyed puppy...

"Ooh is that a Sandwich?"

'Hey Sugar, fancy meeting me in a quiet corner of the cabin? I'll bring the Barry White tunes".

"Hey there! Can't you see me jumping? Is anyone going to lift me up on the couch so I can see what's going on?"

"Treats! Treats! Treats! Dinner! Breakfast! Second breakfast, please....the first wasn't big enough! Treats!"

"Is it time for lunch?"

"Are we going for a car ride? Will there be a MacDonalds on the way?"

"Lil Kim, you lookin' mighty fine gurrrrlll...mmmm hmmmmm"

From the minute he got here, Donald knew he had hit the jackpot and decided to make every moment count.

As much a sex pest as any frisky young adolescent, Donald got a thorough dressing down many, many times those first weeks from Lab mix 'Head Girl' at the cabin, Lil Kim, who let him know without a doubt that her booty was OFF LIMITS.

Did it stop him? Did it heck! He just regrouped, changed tactics, and set his sights a little lower, on to Cairn/ Dachshund mix Trudy, who was much lower to the ground and way easier going!

God only knows what he got up to at the cabin when everyone left for the night.......many times I've been awakened by the sound of seventies porn type soundtracks, and seen a glitter ball or two through the window.

Eh...what are you gonna do?

Last summer we decided to take the risky step of dental surgery in order to prolong his life, as the bacteria in his mouth was not-so-slowly killing him.

Our veterinarians told us he would have weeks left at the most if we didn't do something, and we couldn't bear to not give him that chance of life.

During the surgery, which thankfully was a huge success, we also had his 'chesticle' removed, a bittersweet moment to be honest, because this thing had become such a part of his personality.

So much so that one of our volunteers, Kathy Kohlhagen, even made a brassiere for it, to hold it up off the ground while he walked in the woods.

That little scrap of green Lycra remains in our memorial cabinet to this day.

The 'chesticle' was gone, but never forgotten. RIP.

Donald was not just a valued team member for our community outreach program, his personality was an awesome tool in banishing the blues from every new dog that came in through the doors, all of them sad and bereft at having been dumped by their families at this twilight time of their lives.

His jokey manner and tender companionship earned him a spot at the side of all the newbies....especially Errol Flynn the Chihuahua, and his 'brother from another mother'. The two of them played, cuddled, gossiped and used their film star good looks to keep spirits light at the cabin; they could often be found curled up in a ball together on a huge, blanket covered bed, exhausted from all their exploits.

Over the last few weeks, he has played less and less, and slept more and more. He suffered from a bout of pancreatitis at Christmas which wouldn't go away, no real surprise to anyone who knew the state of his internal organs, but we were just not used to seeing him less than vibrant.

Daily subcutaneous fluids were given by staff members but after a while even that didn't help to perk him up. Over the last few days, his decline was dramatic.

Poor Donald started to have seizures, was unsettled, he paced and whined at times and finally, his breathing became painful after eating.

Yesterday, he lost his sight and then his appetite started to wane......totally unheard of for Donald, who, even with pancreatitis, would try and burgle the fridge.

It was time, we knew it, he knew it, and he wanted us to help the pain go away. We called the veterinary hospital, who arranged for him to be put down at the cabins among his friends, thank God.

So, after having a final snack of chicken nuggets and some cheeseburger, Donald stuck his head in a bowl of his favorite softened cookies while the needle went in, and he drifted away to that great big All You Can Eat buffet in the sky, with a full mouth and loving arms around him.

Donald's last words were "Nom Nom Nom Nom", and that's exactly what he wanted.

His friends, all bar one, stayed in the cabin as he departed: Boris Karloff came over to sniff, (and to see if he'd left any of his packed lunch behind) Jules the Boston Terrier came to lick his snout and his neck, Errol Flynn clambered over his body for a little while before realizing that his friend had gone home, and then sat in a lap close to his pal, just watching and trying to make sense of it all.

Volunteer Kathy Kohlhagen dispensed treats and kisses to keep the coast clear while the final procedure was taking place, and then came to kiss him on his nose and rub his dear old head. I held his head and kissed his nose as he slipped away.

It was peaceful, even if it felt like we were being robbed.

And Little Kim? She stayed outside and gave her 'wannabe paramour' his space, watching from a distance and then as soon as he had left the building, she came back inside to check on her brood and provide a calming presence amid their sadness.

We are so happy for Donald...happy that he got to live here

and to experience such love and peace, and fun. The cabin gave him a new lease of life, a new forever family and a new sense of purpose.

We are happy that he got to spread his particular brand of love to everyone who met him...young, old, infirm, disabled, troubled and lonely.

Most of all, though, we are happy that he got to pass in comfort, when he was ready...a happening reserved for few pups of his age and health.

The legacy he leaves us with is one of determination...to go on, to continue his work, to find another needy senior dog to continue his mission and take his space in the cabin, but never his place in our hearts.

There is one spot in all of our hearts that is long, low, lumpy and beautiful.

It's called Donald's spot, and it'll be there til' the end of time.

FAREWELL TO TALLULAH BANKHEAD, OUR VERY OWN SUNSHINE GIRL

APRIL 2020

On the 15th of April, 2020, we lost Tallulah Bankhead.

Yep, that beautiful girl with the three legs and the sunshine smile……that one.

It's an epic loss for the cabin, and for our volunteer family, because honestly, we just thought she could weather any storm, that she'd be around for a good while longer.

Saying that does sound ridiculous, even to myself, when you think that her body was riddled, yes literally, riddled with cancer, but even though her cancer was huge, it never, ever slowed her down, never defined who she was.

Tallulah, or Toots, as we called her, was a very unique dog from the get-go.

We first met her at Barrow County Animal Control when we went to look at another dog, a big 12 year-old lab called Henry, who just proved to be too energetic and way too 'jumpy' for the calm, easy going senior cabin.

Well, turns out Henry had a sister, sadly separated from her family in the smaller dog section, nevertheless there she was, wagging her tail furiously at us as we walked by the pen saying "Hello there! I'm available. Pick me! Pick me!"

We were looking for a bigger dog, a nice lab who the old folks on our community visits wouldn't have to bend down to pet, but we just couldn't get that girl out of our minds.

Her freshness, her open and honest face, her easy-going demeanour, everything about her screamed Frankie and Andy's Place.

To be honest, she wasn't even really old enough to be there... we are pretty sure she 'faked her passport' by maybe painting in some grey muzzle hairs just before we turned up, but by the time we got an age on her from the vets, we had already committed to her, already fallen in love with that helicopter tail and those bright shining eyes.

Her story was awful; she, her brother Henry and another brother all lived out in the yard 24/7, three hundred and sixty five days a year, in blistering summers, freezing winters, with no respite from the elements.

Dad was a hardened drug dealer who got busted by the Police and was sent to jail. The day he did, Mum took all three dogs and dumped them at the shelter saying she didn't 'want to be messed with the three of them', never had, and now that her husband was in jail, they needed to be gone. She dropped them off and didn't even say goodbye. The staff explained that this could mean they would be euthanized as they were seniors and they were so stretched for room, but she didn't bat an eyelid.

For one of the dogs, that woman's decision was fatal. Very nervous and highly reactive, Toots' brother stayed at Barrow County Animal shelter for an age while the staff desperately searched for a home for him, until, thanks to sheer numbers, they no longer could.

Henry, the lab we originally went to meet, went to a rescue who had a decent home lined up, with land where he could bounce around all day like Tigger.

And Toots? Well, Toots hit the bloody jackpot didn't she?

She ran in to the cabins that first day, excitedly greeting everyone, jumped up on the table that we had near to the fence and hopped right over into the woods!

Ummm...what just happened??? Seriously?

But...but...we thought she was a senior!

We realized then and there that we had a little pistol on our hands, so we moved all the furniture into the center of the yard and shored up the fence a bit.

We needn't have worried, by the end of the week she had worked out that the chicken casserole and beef pot roast was THIS side of the fence and she never tried to escape again.

Watching her live out her freedom fantasy after 10 or 11 years of being chained up in a back yard was the stuff dreams are made of. The first one to greet us in the morning, running outside with a hop and a skip, always ready to wrestle with cabin 'Head Boy' Boris, always impatient to go somewhere.

At night she would go find a corner and bark at imaginary dragons. Years of protecting her yard never left her, not even when she had a cosy bed inside to lay on.

Toots just loved to be out, loved to feel the fresh breeze on her body, to raise her nose and inhale the scents on the air.

She was like that right until the end.

We find this so often with previously outside dogs; they find it hard getting used to the comforts of indoors sometimes. Toots' best day was a run, a good meal and a Kurunda bed on the porch, especially in the winter when she'd be swaddled in a blanket, breathing in the crisp, cold air.

When she came to us, she had a growth on her leg, which grew little by little 'til it became the size of a golf ball and oddly cauliflower-esque.

We didn't mess with it, our cabin is palliative care only and also, we don't always agree with cutting away cancer, because that sometimes has an adverse effect. It can be that by opening up the body for surgery, we are oxygenating and breathing fuel into the very thing we are trying to kill. We tread carefully with cancer, we respect it always but we do not ever give it an opportunity to thrive.

As always, we decided to monitor and concentrate on wellness, building the immune system and treating the whole dog.

It worked for a massive two and a half years and then, when she was thirteen and a half, that thing just started to balloon and get infected.

Her veterinarian debrided the tumor multiple times, but the effects were short lived.

They advised us to cut the leg off, telling us "This is one cool dog, we think she can conquer this", but because by this time her X-rays showed she had other cancer sites, more worryingly, a number of tumors in her chest, I didn't want to.

I wish I'd listened to them in this case.

When that tumor on her leg ruptured, and the infection was the thing that was going to take her life, and not the cancer, I finally decided to go ahead. She was otherwise so 'well', you see…without that infection no one would guess she had this beast growing inside of her.

It took her a good while to recover, but I'm happy to say that it was the right decision.

Once she got used to walking on three legs, Toots popped right back to where she had been, happy, tail wagging and up for anything.

Like I said, I wish I'd done it sooner. I'd give anything to turn back the clock but of course hindsight is 20/20.

In my mind, I was desperately hoping for six more good months for her; I told the vets I'd be happy with four, but six would be wonderful.

Almost six months to the week, she started to go downhill very rapidly.

The metastasized tumors in her lungs impaired her breathing, she stopped eating, went into organ failure and couldn't even raise her body temperature to fight whatever was going on. That's why we had to make the awful decision to say goodbye.

Oh God, it's so hard when you know it's the right and only decision but then the selfish side of you says "But can't we just….?" and as always, "What if….?"

But I'm not going to concentrate on that, I'm just thinking

about that extra six months of lush, vibrant life force that she brought to the cabin.

I'd go through all of that again, all of us would, to have her for even one more week, such was her ability to grasp life and live it to the full.

She was a veritable powerhouse of joy, like sunshine in a spray bottle.

Her face lit up the room, her tail wag sent us all into realms of delight and not one of our volunteers failed to rush to see her at the cabin when they found out she was home from surgery.

Four legs or three, no matter.

She conquered her world, our world, and brought us all three and a half years of total happiness.

Thank you, sweet Tallulah. From the bottom of our hearts, we want you to know the effect you had on us all and how you changed our lives.

'Toots' taught us so much about overcoming adversity, and her legacy will live on in this Frankie and Andy's Place Family of volunteers and staff forever.

Nighty Night little girl.

FAREWELL TO HOLLY HUNTER, SHE CAME, SHE SAW, SHE KICKED PLENTY OF ASS

MARCH 2022

On January 26th, the cabin door opened and in strutted Holly Hunter.

She'd clearly stopped on the way to buy herself a set of stilts, attached them to her legs, snagged herself a big bag of attitude, and oh boy, she was dead set on using both!

This teeny-tiny little girl was a bit of a train wreck.

She had been saved by our friends at Releash Atlanta who

had placed her in foster care with our amazing volunteer Cynthia Barrett, who 'double dips' to help both of our organizations... Cynthia is an angel, for sure.

Holly was not thriving though; she had a bad chest infection, she wasn't eating, her weight was dropping and her kidneys were shot. At under four pounds, even an ounce can make the difference between viable and non-viable and so Releash Atlanta quickly realized how knife-edge this was, and that this girl needed some specialist care throughout her last days. So we offered to have her for hospice care at Frankie and Andy's Place and hoped for even a few weeks with this delightful, super sassy little girl.

Every day, she had to have fluids and vitamin B12 subcutaneously, which, gotta be honest, she was more than a bit of a pain in the ass for...

A feisty dog in hospice care, though, is a wonderful thing. It shows their spirit isn't gone and that there's plenty of fight left, but dear God, it's no fun for our poor staff who felt like they were going into the lion's den every day.

One look at the fluids bag and she'd start Kung fu fighting. Full-on Bruce Lee in 'Fist of fury'.

We had team members asking for back-up, enquiring if there any chance of a security detail, even trying to book the Delta Force and Seal Team 6 for combat support...it was crazy.

But that little girl endured and kept fighting and fighting and fighting...doing everything on her terms.

She wouldn't eat.

Well, okay, that's not strictly true, what I mean is, she refused to eat any of OUR delightful, freshly cooked, home-made gourmet food with succulent meats, vegetables and herbs.

Oh no, that girl decided from the get-go that she was only going to eat McDonalds, and even then it had to be freshly cooked. "Nuh uh, don't be trying to fool me with no frozen McDonalds stash, I ain't takin' that on! I want FRESH!"

Oh, and as for food service? "Hand feeding only, please, my good woman, I'm too posh to eat from a bowl".

And so it was that every day, Ranch Manager Aunty Kris would go buy her a fresh set of cheeseburgers, nuggets, or whatever she wanted.

Those of you out there in our Frankie and Andy's Place supporter family must be scratching your head and thinking, "Why on earth would they feed her that? It's not good for her!"

Of course it wasn't.

But, let's be honest, what was it going to do...kill her?

She was in hospice care and at that point, we badly needed her to eat or she'd die, but just way sooner and without a smile on her face.

Always, our mission is to make them happy for as long as they have. Sometimes that means breaking all the rules.

Holly was the consummate Naomi Campbell/dirty little street fighter mix, with those long, long legs and her 'hang tough' attitude. She provided us with 6 weeks of entertainment, education and moments of pure hilarity.

Every volunteer and care team member at Frankie and Andy's Place is lamenting her loss.

Each one of them wishes she'd had longer, if only because she was SO MUCH FUN!

Earlier this week, in a complete 180 to how she lived, Holly Hunter left us peacefully.

Curled up in her blankets, not a thing out of place, Holly

passed quietly in her sleep with a calmness and serenity that was totally unexpected. A staff member found her in the early morning, and was heartbroken, but also relieved at the peace she instantly felt in her heart that Holly had gone in the way we'd all wish to.

Holly Hunter was like a comet.

A big flash that blazed across the sky, commanded everyone's attention, illuminated the world with her HUGE presence and then Poof! She was gone.

I think she meant it to be that way.

I'd like to say "Rest In Peace, Holly Hunter", but I doubt it's anything but calm and peaceful up there if she's arrived!

So instead, let's say "You go girl! Do your thing and whip 'em all into shape!"

FAREWELL TO KIEFER SUTHERLAND 'HE AIN'T HEAVY, HE'S MY BROTHER'

AUGUST 2021

I put off writing this eulogy for a whole week because every time I put my fingers on the keyboard, it all seemed too real and I just didn't want it to.

Writing a eulogy makes it official...like there's no going back, even though of course, I know that's ridiculous as there isn't any way back from loss.

Certainly not a loss this huge...

Kiefer Sutherland is no longer with us.

The beautiful little lamb who came in as 'Old Man Toothless' and left as a megastar with a following of thousands upon thousands who swooned over his every picture, passed away last Tuesday.

Even though he was 17 years of age, and had been battling ill health for some time, as we shared on this page a month or so ago, this actually hit us like a train.

He was in congestive heart failure, and the meds that were saving his life by pulling the fluid from his lungs were actually dehydrating him to the point that he started to have seizures.

It's one of those 'damned if you do, damned if you don't' situations that we as a canine hospice facility face every day.

However, with some clever tinkering on the part of our incredible team, who stayed with him day and night, visited with him, wrapping him in arms of love, they were able to get him over that hump and bring him back to us, so that he and his very best buddy Justin Timberlake, a tiny and timid Yorkshire Terrier otherwise known as JT, could snuggle together once more.

It's hard getting old, but so much easier when you have a good friend by your side. JT came to us with a broken heart and a shy, cautious approach to relationships. In Kiefer he saw not only a kindred spirit, but someone who could accompany him on his journey through the often rough pathway of navigating old age. Kiefer was by his side after JT lost his leg, urging him to keep smiling, keep fighting...

At a time when we feared he may not make it, Kiefer was there assuring him he could do this, he'd be there for him.

A selfless little old man who saw his job in life was to bolster and uplift those around him...you can only imagine how JT is reeling from this humongous loss.

But today, I am not going to focus so much on the incredible yawning chasm of loss that this boy leaves behind.

No, today I am going to focus on the power that one tiny little 5 pound poodle with ears like Yoda, eyes that saw little but, in fact, saw everything and legs that looked like someone had attached stilts to them, kindly wielded over the mission of Frankie and Andy's Place.

With one tilt of his head, this boy moved people from tears to smiles.

With one comic stumble on the back deck, this boy had the audience in the palm of his hand, and in the early days used to ham it up shamelessly.

One touch of that soft, lamb-like fur transported our volunteers into raptures of delight.

One nuzzle into a neck as he dozed meant no-one was moving, so precious was a moment like that, and so restorative for the recipient.

A natural on school visits, Kiefer took to the task like a natural, quickly becoming the doggy of choice at Oakwood elementary school back in 2020 when we started to do classroom visits with the special needs children there.

Happy to sit and listen as they read, Kiefer was the perfect teacher's assistant and everyone wanted him for their classroom.

At the Adult Daycare Center, Kiefer allowed himself to be touched and held by anyone who needed a slice of his particular brand of empathy.

He was like a love train…you couldn't hold him back, he gave and gave of himself selflessly on every week's visit because he just enjoyed his gift and the effect it had on anyone in his orbit.

Kiefer was born to love others.

PENNY MILLER

From his cabin mates, to our volunteers, to anyone he met on community visits.....it was like being anointed by a celestial being.

He was the most powerful, tiny being we ever knew and a true brother to everyone in the FAAP family.

If ever there was a song written for one single soul, it was the famous sixties song by The Hollies, 'He ain't heavy, he's my brother'.

> **The road is long**
> **With many a winding turn**
> **That leads us to who knows where, who knows where**
> **But I'm strong**
> **Strong enough to carry him**
> **He ain't heavy, he's my brother"**

Goodbye old friend, we have loved you....and will always continue to love you.

You shone a light on our mission, and in our hearts.

Rest In Peace, beautiful boy.

FAREWELL TO GRACE OUR VERY OWN 'AMAZING GRACE'

SEPTEMBER 2023

Just like a shooting star, she lit up the sky for a brief moment in time, and then she was gone, leaving all in her wake aghast at her splendor, her light, her sheer impact...

Grace, our beautiful Springer Spaniel hospice resident, entrusted to us for her final weeks by the wonderful Gwinnett Jail Dogs Program, passed away a few days ago, and we are still reeling from her loss.

When we first heard about Grace and her diagnosis, we jumped at the chance to have her at the cabins.

PENNY MILLER

As you may know, she was just a young thing, anywhere from 3 to 6 years of age depending on which vet you listen to, and way, way younger than any of our other pups. But, we are a senior dog sanctuary AND hospice care facility and so any dog nearing the end of its' life, and looking for a soft landing, is welcome with us.

Thankfully, we work so closely with The Society of Humane Friends and Gwinnett Jail Dogs Program, that they automatically know our criteria for intake, and so when they asked us if we could help, we jumped at the chance.

And oh boy, what a gift this was…not just for us humans who got to meet the sweetest of souls, but for the dogs at the cabins, who enjoyed her kind, gentle spirit and unfettered joy at life.

"Whoa, is that chicken casserole? With REAL big chunks of chicken? Load me up!"

"Ummm, is that toast for me? And is that butter? Oh boy, this so cool!"

"So hang on, three big meals a day, cookies, AND toast with butter on demand? Ay Caramba! Woo Hoo!"

That Swiffer Sweeper of a tail was wagging so violently at mealtimes we thought she'd fall over, she was so excited. But this angel was always patient and kind around the other dogs when they were waiting to receive their food.

After meals, and after her nose had been put to the test in the wooded yard outside, which she adored, she would go find her boyfriend big white German Shepherd Hugh Jackman, himself another Society of Humane Friends Alumni, and snuggle into the warmth of his presence.

Two beautiful souls thrown together by destiny and choosing to stick together like glue simply because they saw themselves in each other.

Every day, Grace would wake up and just decide to live her best life.

Simple as that.

And how amazingly wonderful is that?

We know so many humans who obsess about small inconsequential things, but Grace, the girl whose days were numbered, didn't just see the crescent, she saw the whole of the moon.

Every butterfly was a friend to play chase with, every bird was a song to listen to and every scent on the breeze was a promise of great things to come. Every lap was there to be laid in and every hand was a harbinger of joy. There was not a volunteer in our 40 strong 'Love Army' who didn't think that they were her absolute favorite after the first meeting, she made them all feel so special. I have used this phrase before and I unashamedly use it again, they all felt 'touched by an Angel'.

She was perfection.

But like a stunning Georgia Day Lily, Grace's time was short. She bloomed and bloomed and then abruptly her petals dropped.

And that is what happened last weekend.

In the morning, she was happily lounging on the deck with one of her 'besties', Graham Nash, and then suddenly, without warning, at 8pm that night, after a good dinner and a nap, she started to seize violently and this continued for over two minutes.

When she came to us, we researched her condition of Hepatic Encelopathy and knew that eventually seizures may come, and that blindness may also happen. What we didn't expect was for both to appear at the same time and render her, post seizure, going between catatonic and staggering blindly for three hours. We feared the worst and made preparations to get her to the emergency vet hospital, but then she suddenly popped up, felt better and kissed her Aunty Jen.

"Phew" we thought, "She is going to make it. This was just a minor setback. We have time with her, still".

Quickly, we let our friends at Gwinnett Jail Dogs Program know what was going on and asked that they let her Jail handler know to be prepared, that it could be any day.

Three hours later, as suddenly and as out of nowhere as the one before, she experienced another seizure, but this one lasted for eight minutes.

Experience has shown us that there is no coming back from a seizure this long, the body's temperature gets too high and the brain basically fries. So, even before the seizure stopped, we knew that the disease had become uncontainable, like a wildfire.

Our team members Aunty Jen and Uncle Michael lifted her into the car and drove her down to the emergency vets, where they gently let her go, after first wrapping her in their arms and telling her how beautiful, how kind she was and thanking her for her perfect service.

She never woke up again after that monstrous 8 minute seizure, she was already gone in all but her beating heart.

This is one of the saddest cases we have ever had and yet conversely, one of the most joyful.

We do not believe in coincidence at Frankie and Andy's Place; we believe that every soul arrives on our doorstep for a reason, and this bringer of joy certainly did her job in the mere twenty days that she was with us.

We feel so honored that Gwinnett Jail Dogs and The Society of Humane Friends of Georgia, who partner with us in so many ways, chose us to spend the final chapter with this delightful soul.

Every day, every moment, was a joy.

Her unfettered enthusiasm for everything in sight was a lesson in life to us all.

Thank you so much for this incredible opportunity to have Grace, know Grace, and feel Grace....surely the most aptly named dog on the planet.

Rest in peace little one, sleep tight.

FAREWELL TO FRANNIE THE WONDER DOG, WHO STOLE OUR HEARTS

APRIL 2019

On Wednesday morning, one of the greatest dogs to ever come through these doors, 'Frannie the Wonder-Dog', lost her fight and passed over the bridge.

Frannie was stunningly beautiful, amazingly stubborn, strong as an ox and funny as shit!

This delightful little girl, who came to us in 2017 with completely crippled back legs, bladder stones, severe arthritis in one leg and a dislocated elbow in the other was the living embodiment of 'The Little Engine that could.'

We weren't looking for another dog at the cabin, we were at full complement...but then Chandler Riddett from the Society of Humane Friends sent me this picture and I instantly fell head over heels in love with those bright eyes, wispy eyebrows and that lollipop tongue.

I mean it.

Head over heels.

There was no way I was going to say no to this dog, and I'm so glad I didn't.

Little Frannie instantly became the cabin pin-up, schmoozing her way around the group, playful and kind, eager to please everyone she met and oh-so attentive to her new human family.

This little beauty manoeuvred her little body all over the place using just her front legs, exploring the yard at an incredible pace despite her many disabilities.

Turned in by her owners to the County shelter in Dekalb because her physical problems were too much for them to handle, this little girl was snapped up by the Society of Humane Friends who saw more in her in ten seconds than her asshole owners could ever have done. They had her in foster care for a while as they worked on some of her health issues, but knew she would thrive with us.

And boy did she thrive!

In April 2018, this little girl wowed hundreds of people at our annual golf day fund raiser as she bombed around on the beautiful greens at Lake Lanier's Legacy golf course. The sight of her more mobile than she had ever been made us determined that Frannie would have lovely flat grass to run on at home. And so it was that when the new big cabin and surrounds was completed, 'Frannie's Run' was the crowning glory...with yards of glorious, flat, green turf for our girl to jolly around on.

I've never seen so many grown people moved to tears as when we unveiled her new soft 'playground' and watched her skip on her two front legs, ass-bumping her way along, smiling from ear to ear.

Just a perfect moment, that will stay with all of us forever.

That is why I'm not going to dwell too much on the details of how we lost our darling girl, I think we need to hold on to that perfect moment.

Suffice to say, we battled for her life because we couldn't bear the thought of life without her at the cabin, but finally had to admit defeat. Probably long after I should have done, and I honestly don't feel good about that.

I was insanely in love with her and thought "maybe this or that will work" or "maybe this neurological circling with her body is just temporary?"

Of course it wasn't. It was my heart calling the shots when my head should have been instead.

Frannie spent her last day with us down at the Desperate Dogs Ranch, sitting on a donut bed right in the middle of the dining room table as we had our daily 'family time' coffee break. That night she slept beside me in my bed as she had become accustomed of late, and all night I was gazing at her, thinking "She might still be okay".

You see, she had been so many times before.

Our staff used to jokingly shout "Hey Pete and Penny, your girl wants a few weeks down at the Ranch! She's pretending to be under the weather again!"

She'd spend her days with us across the driveway at Desperate Dogs, my husband Pete taking her for gentle stroller rides up and down the driveway and down the street. Then she would lay in the crook of my arms overnight and miraculously recover from anything.....from rabies to a nuclear holocaust blast (okay, slight exaggeration) just by feeling connected, cossetted.

This time, it didn't work.

She was in pain, she was oh-so tired of her little body being so broken and bent and she wanted out.

On Wednesday morning she got her wish and I took her down to our vets, who, as always, took care of her final needs softly and gently.

She slipped away looking into my eyes, grateful and fully aware, speaking softly with no sound.

"Shhhhhh Mum" she said. "I'm ready for the next leg of my journey. I'm okay with this and you need to be too, because that's what love does. Let me sleep now, and tomorrow I will be running and playing in grassy meadows under golden sunlight. I'll wait for you. I will see you again. This is not the end of us, Mum, it's not goodbye."

I cling to that.

Even as I write this, four days after she left us, I'm still clinging to that.

Oh my beautiful, our beautiful, perfect Frannie girl, I loved you before I met you.

We all did.

Nighty night little girl, we will see you on the other side.

FAREWELL TO YOGI BERRA, THE SPECIAL BOY WHO LAUNCHED A MOVEMENT

JULY 2023

On July 25th, the world came crashing down.

We lost Yogi Berra.

Yogi, the beautiful, kind and most perfect of dogs, formerly known as 'Red Dog' on the streets of Atlanta where he lived for 14 years as a beloved companion to his owner, a homeless gentleman, passed away.

A victim to that particularly nasty 'creep-up-on-you' killer,

Hemangiosarcoma, we never saw this coming. We know a thing or two about this condition, but in this case, there were no obvious signs.

He woke up in the morning, and instead of his usual happy go lucky self, he would not eat, would not get up, would not move, and just quietly lay in the office on the floor.

A check of his body temperature showed it to be very low.

A stethoscope to his chest showed a heart rate so fast, but a respiratory rate that was normal.

We knew right away that it was his heart and presumed that some heart meds would see him right, so we rushed him to our local veterinary hospital, who, as always, fitted us in right away.

X-Rays showed there was a mass on his heart, but more concerning, a huge mass on his spleen, and fluid in his lungs. The poor boy could not move, could not eat, because everything was so squished up inside, that tumor was taking up all of the available real estate.

There was simply nothing we could do, we had to let him go.

He passed with his beloved Aunty Jennifer cuddling him, her body wrapped around his, whispering into his ear. She told him that he was the most perfect soul, that he was leaving us covered with the love of thousands of people whose lives he had touched...and that there was even more love waiting for him on the other side.

All of our dogs pass this way, it is a part of our mission, and our promise to them when they arrive.

Yogi Berra was a once in a lifetime dog.

A beautiful tan Pitbull, Yogi's soft face and gentle personality made him the perfect breed ambassador, and a firm favorite with everyone at the cabins.

He could always be found lying or sitting on top of the picnic table, barking happily at the dogs down at the Desperate Dogs Boarding Ranch down the hill, or telling folks to come and pay homage to his gorgeousness.

No one could refuse, he was simply perfect.

Breakfast, lunch and dinner was served, and even hand fed to him, at this table, so that he could enjoy those spring sunshine hours outside in the cabin yard. Or even winter sunshine hours, when he was wrapped in a blanket so he could stay outside in his favorite spot.

Like so many formerly outside dogs, he loved the fresh air and freedom, and needed to drink it in daily. He also loved him a leather armchair or sofa in the cabin lounge to sleep on at night, when his wish for some luxurious home comforts kicked in, but without fail he always needed to be outside during waking hours.

Everyone loved him, and everyone thought he loved them the most...and of course, everyone was right.

For 14 years prior to coming to us, Yogi was best friend, confidante and security detail to a homeless gentleman who lived on the streets of Atlanta.

This kind man gave up life with his best friend in order to save his life. Yogi had a horrific, huge tumor on his testicles that was badly infected and urgently needed removal. The man could not have taken care of him post-surgically, not in those dirty, cruel streets, and so he gave him up, despite knowing it would rob him of his beloved partner.

Such an act of selflessness deserved recognition and so we not only took Yogi Berra in, we decided to honor this man and his canine best friend by helping other dogs and their homeless owners.

It was because of Yogi's story that we decided to launch our "Helping Hands, Healing Paws Outreach" a brand new outreach serving homeless pets and their people, targeting homeless populations in our surrounding cities.

After months of preparation, the new storage building that houses all of the supplies for us to distribute to needy souls was finally delivered. A mere two hours after its' arrival, Yogi glimpsed it as he left the cabins for the last time on his way to the vets, never to return.

'Devastated' doesn't even begin to describe it, and yet, for those of us who mourn his loss, we have all come to the same conclusion.

He was sent to us on a mission of his own, to raise awareness and highlight a need, and to be an inspiration for our next initiative.

Because of this beautiful red dog, whose story has been shared near and far, thousands of people see Pit Bulls differently. Thousands of people have a different view of the plight of the homeless and the disadvantaged, and now many, many street dogs and their owners, as well as local rescues and shelters, will get the help they need.

It is as if Yogi was hanging on to make sure we followed through on our promise, and then knew he could let go once he saw that we had.

Farewell, sweet Yogi Berra, and thank you for gracing this little paradise of ours...we will never forget you, and we will work hard to honor you in the legacy you leave behind.

PENNY MILLER

Every street dog will know that the gifts we distribute will be through, and because of you. We hope desperately to meet your former owner out there, so that he can see what a good thing he did when he selflessly gave you up so you could get the help you needed.

Well done, beautiful boy, well done...such a good dog.

Time to Rest In Peace now.

FAREWELL TO OLIVIA NEWTON JOHN, A BUNDLE OF LOVE AND JOY IN A DOG'S BODY

MAY 2021

5,270,400 seconds.

That's what we were told she had.

Seems a lot doesn't it?

But it's actually 60 days.

Just 60 days.

It was tough to hear, especially as this delightful blocky-headed beauty had already spent the last 248 days at the Barrow

County Shelter, where she had resided in a concrete run, rarely seeing the sunlight on her face or hearing the birds sing.

The shelter is tough on the old ones, with no soft surface to lie on and a dedicated but overworked staff who do as much as they can.....but it's certainly no Hilton.

We met Olivia Newton John, formerly known as Vera, one sunny September day when Ranch Manager Kris Snyder and I went to the shelter to evaluate another dog as a possible candidate for the sanctuary and asked if there were any calm dogs there that we could use for his temperament test.

Out walked this stocky 75 pound Pitty girl, waddling along like she was carrying ten bags of groceries on each hip, tail wagging fiercely from side to side and smiling politely.

She performed beautifully on the temperament test; we really liked her, but we only had room for one, so the dog we went to see came home with us as we had already committed to him and she sadly remained at the shelter.

It almost killed us to leave her.

Every time we talked over the next few days, Kris and I would mention her and wish we had a spot for her, we'd giggle about her wiggle and feel sick at how long she had been incarcerated......until finally, one day, we thought "Screw this", and decided to just bite the bullet and get her, even though we were full.

Our first stop is always the animal hospital so that our oldies can get checked over, and it was there, on that X-Ray table, that I heard those words "two months tops" from our veterinarian.

She had a large tumor on her spleen that was so big other vets were coming in to see it on the screen and shaking their heads sadly. The light gray football shape in her stomach was so easy to spot on the screen that even I could work out what it was and gulped.

"'Jesus" I said.

Followed by, "Holy Shit".

Even the vet said he was thinking the EXACT same thing.

Surgery wasn't an option.....it was too risky, that bloody thing ('Alien' as we called it) was just too big and she was too old, so we decided that with 60 days or so, we had better get her busy living or get her busy dying.

We chose living!

We introduced her to cabin life and she right from the get-go was overjoyed!

Skin like sandpaper with the mange, big chunks of hot red moist pustulous patches all over her body with the allergies, arthritic limbs that made her move like a wooden doll, Olivia was a hot mess, but yet a happy one.

She soaked up the sun like it was the wellspring of life, she kindly met all the other cabin residents and settled happily on soft beds, patiently being sprayed down with antibiotic sprays or having creams rubbed into her sore spots. She never complained, never grumbled although it can't have been pleasant. She just smiled and looked grateful.

A week or so after she got to us, her whole life changed in an instant.

She met the love of her life, Kelly Mitchell, one of our volunteer angels, and she decided right there and then, that she was going to do anything she could, just to live long enough to be with her.

As Kelly left that day, Olivia cried.

When Kelly heard her soulful whining, she came back to kiss her on the head and say one last goodbye, and Olivia danced a happy dance.

From that day forth, she checked her schedule, set her watch and was sure to be right there at the gate when Kelly arrived.

Days turned into weeks and, after 4 or five months, we watched her jumping around at the gate for her beloved Kelly to come in and suddenly realized, "Hey, she's been here quite a long while now, and she's STILL doing great!"

When I call Olivia a miracle girl later in this piece, I am going to pre-qualify that right now by saying that the miracle was borne out of her love for Kelly.

We all need something to live for, and Kelly was Olivia's thing, her purpose.

Every time she walked in, Olivia's sun, moon and stars would rise in the sky and she would howl with happiness.

Together they enjoyed the crisp, golden leaves on autumnal days, Olivia rolling around like a puppy, giddy with delight.

Kelly would take her for long car rides in her Jeep, Olivia on the back seat, eyes always fixed on Kelly instead of looking out of the window.

Somehow Olivia always managed to talk Kelly into a McDonalds stop off on the way home, and the two of them would trot back in through the gates with bags of swag for the others. Olivia's hamster cheeks would be brimming with nugget pieces, as she swore blind she hadn't had any treats.....ced"Nom Nom, Slurp, Nom Nom".

Community visits, cabin visitors, special needs children visiting from the local school, Olivia was everybody's friend and the perfect therapy dog.

Her trademark waddle combined with her white socks and sing-song voice made her irresistible.

Plenty of people have come to the cabin frightened of Pit bulls and been shown the error of their ways by this beautiful girl.

She was astonishingly kind, incredibly sensitive…and our proudest achievement thus far.

We started Frankie and Andy's Place Senior Dog Sanctuary in May 2015.

Our aim was to re-write the final chapter for neglected, abused, forlorn dogs who had been cruelly cast aside by their former owners. We just wanted to give them a perfect forever home and re-right past injustices.

We decided to put our faith in palliative care, love and kindness as a medicine, and good food as a healer. The gift of time was always going to be the most important thing we could bestow.

From September 2018, when that gorgeous girl waddled into our lives, until she passed on May 2nd 2021, that girl soaked up every single bit she could of all we had to give. Then she gift wrapped it and returned it to us tenfold.

When that tumor had become so large that poor Olivia just couldn't find comfort any more, we asked Kelly if she would like to be the one to take her for her final vet visit. Heart breaking and stomach twisted into knots, she agreed, knowing that this was to be her final, but greatest gift to the girl she loved so well.

Kelly held her beautiful big head in her hands and kissed her gently on her brow, while the vet took care of her final needs.

Kelly tells us that Olivia knew she had to go, knew her body had passed its use-by date, but that she was okay with this because her beloved was with her, smiling into her eyes, a guiding light for the next stage of her journey.

Olivia was a miracle of faith and a miracle of love.

It is because of this and this alone, that those 60 days turned into a whopping 972.

Yes.....972 days.

That's 23,328 hours.

83,980,800 seconds.

And she lived every single one to the fullest.

God bless that beautiful girl, and may we all utter a huge thank you for her life and smile.

Man, what a precious soul she was.

Rest In Peace Olivia, sleep tight now beautiful girlie.

FAREWELL TO DAVID BECKHAM, WHO HAD US AT 'HELLO'

SEPTEMBER 2020

While we obviously welcome, love, and ultimately say farewell to many dogs at Frankie and Andy's Place, some leave a more indelible mark than others.

Such a dog was David Beckham, who left us after a long battle with failing health.

David started having seizures after a very bad infection took hold of him in 2019 and, even though he regained his vast appetite and some, but not all, of his 'joie de vivre', he was never quite the same afterwards.

David passed at the Ranch, in the arms of our Ranch Manager Aunty Kristen, aided gently by our 'Florence Nightingale' dog, Busy Phillips.

Was he a sweet old gentleman?

Well, I'm going to start by telling you that a few months after David arrived at the cabins, we had a serious meeting about that boy because by then we were all sure he'd faked his passport to get in, like a number of his predecessors.

Imagine if you will...... Robin Williams with all his cheeky charm, personality and gregarious physicality, then add the innocence and sweetness of Gandhi, toss in a huge dollop of juggling circus clown and round it off with a touch of Adam Richman from 'Man versus Food' (you know, the show where the guy goes around the US finding wonderful restaurants to eat himself sick at) you come pretty close to who David Beckham was.

Meh, maybe times that by 10! Yeah, that's more like it.

David came to us in 2018 from Peach County Animal Rescue, survivor of a harrowing situation. The local Police begged them to take him in and help him after he was found during a traffic stop, in a van, along with 18 or so other animals. A few of those animals were dead, and had been for some time.

Let the horror of that sink in for a moment...

Peach County took wonderful care of his initial needs, saw that he was an absolute poppet but that he would need some specialized care, so they asked if we could take him.

With our background in behavioral rehab, we knew that David would take a fair bit of time to realize he was now safe, and we also knew that the way to heal him from his past was to crowd out the awful memories with wonderful, happy new ones. We of course said 'yes' right away.

And so it began......

First, he needed a fabulous new name; it had to be perfect, so we gave that very important task to Jessie Johnson, our 15 year-old intern, who thought he would look just gorgeous when he was a bit chunkier, and so David Beckham he became.

Then, up stepped the rest of the FAAP family of volunteers and staff, who made it their mission in life to love him, cosset him, take him for walks in the woods and tell him at every opportunity that he was the sexiest beast on the planet. It didn't take him long to start feeling like an Arab Sheikh with his own harem of doting women.

Of course, he needed a new diet....we needed to get weight on him pretty fast as he had 'xylophone ribs' even after Peach County had been feeding him up.

We used a careful diet of meat, fish, some vegetables, brown rice pasta, eggs, raw goats milk and even buttermilk at times to help him gain weight.

It worked a treat. David became a big fat tick within just a few months.

Although it has to be said, our idea of a big fat tick was different to his.

We said "Okay chunky monkey, you're getting to be a bit of a porker, we can slow down on the food now".

David on the other hand was like "Nuh-uhh, I ain't done yet, Sister, Imma try and be the world's first 20 inch tall hippopotamus!"

Dear God there was no stopping the little scallywag....we needed to erect large barriers around anywhere that food was cooked, stored or served, as we quickly realized that David could jump anything, push through anything, open anything and EAT anything, if the flight of fancy took him.

And it did take him...every minute he was awake! Pretty sure he sleep-walked into the pantry a few times for a nosh, as food items went missing overnight occasionally, but the other dogs provided alibis for him every time. Hmmmm...

We have a picture beside the window in the kitchen of the big cabin. It's of David, situated right outside the window looking in at one of our staff preparing dinner. He was actually standing on a full height dining table that he had jumped up on to in order to stalk our chefs as they worked.

13 years old he was back then, and he was like a bloody mountain goat!

His hilarious antics made us have hyper-angst and, at the same time, collapse with fits of giggles.

He'd infuriate you by knocking over the gate that separates the kitchen from the rest of the cabin, stick his whole head in the trash bucket looking for scraps and then be forced to walk around with it on his head because it would get stuck! If you've ever seen the movie 'Parenthood' where the kid gets the bucket stuck on his head, you'll picture the scene with ease.

We always pulled the bucket off of him, ready to say "Dear God, David..really?????" and he'd fix us with those soulful eyes, that one fang-like tooth curling up into his upper lip like a stumpy caramelized sugar lump, and no one, but NO ONE, could resist him.

Every single volunteer, every single member of staff had a 'thing' for David.

Every single person felt that they were his favorite, that they alone had an incredible connection with him...and you know what? Every single one of them was right!

He had the unique knack of making you feel like you were his one and only.

God, we shall miss him.

They broke the mold when they made him and no mistake.

So, if all is right and proper, David will, right about now, be sitting down to a big barbecued whole cow with a side of fries, ten thousand chicken nuggets from Chick Fil A, a couple hundred pork tenderloins, a big plate of sausages, maybe some liver pate...

"Oh, and Garçon? ...I'd better have a few boxes of those delicious Three Dog bakery cookies too for dessert."

"Coming right up, David," the angels will be saying, because in truth, no one ever could resist 'Becks'.

They will be eating out of his perfect little paws up there like Posh Spice.

Nighty Night Precious boy, Rest In Peace.

WELCOME TO MEEMAW, FOR AS LONG AS WE CAN ENJOY YOU

NOVEMBER 2020

Today, we are breaking with tradition and announcing a new arrival who only just got to the cabin yesterday afternoon.

We normally wait for a couple of weeks so that 'freshmen' have time to settle in and for one of our volunteers to get to name them appropriately; however, due to the circumstances, this resident will keep the name that she has come to us with....

Ladies and Gentlemen we are delighted to introduce you to Meemaw, a beautiful senior golden lab with a heart of gold.

Sadly for Meemaw, she also has a heart full of heartworms and is in a very bad way. Her time with us is not likely to be long as she is struggling to breathe and her body is exhausted. She was callously dumped at the shelter after years of neglect by an owner knowing that she would be put to sleep.

An owner who dumped her anyway...

The shelter she was in were desperate for someone to take this girl because of her loving personality and kind ways, and were devastated when not one rescue showed interest in her. All were concerned about the cost of treatment and the lack of hope, knowing she was a hospice case.

At Frankie and Andy's Place, however, where others fear to tread, we go boldly...

Our incredible staff and volunteers spring into action for cases like this and make it their number one priority to ensure that Meemaw, from this moment on, will know love, kindness; her days, no matter how few they will be, until the minute she draws her very last breath, will be guaranteed to be like this.

What was once cast away as someone else's trash, has now become our most highly prized treasure and we consider it our incredible privilege to care for her.

We will keep you posted along the way, but for now we ask for your prayers that this beautiful, gentle soul can keep on breathing and allow the cabin to work its' magic.

We have worked many miracles at Frankie and Andys's Place.

We also have faith in the power of love and kindness.

Please pray for Meemaw today and welcome her into your heart as we welcome her into our beautiful cabin home.

FAREWELL TO MEEMAW, AN ANGEL WHO CAME DOWN TO EARTH, AND ENDED UP STAYING A WHILE

FEBRUARY 2022

'In the arms of an angel, fly away from here...'

On Friday, God called Meemaw, the most perfect dog on the entire planet, home.

"My perfect child" He said to her, "I sent you down to live on earth so that people would experience love and gentleness, so that they would find beauty and peace in a time of chaos and sadness. But heaven has missed its' most flawless of angels, your work there is done, it's time for you to come home."

And so it was, that on late Friday afternoon, Meemaw's heart stopped beating...and the world was instantly darker.

Heaven's gain was our devastating loss.

Meemaw came to us from Lee County Humane Society in Auburn, Alabama. One of their incredible volunteers, Jill, reached out to me in November of 2020 and asked if we had room for this kindly old Golden Lab to spend her final days.

Her body battered by years of neglect, heartworms and the chronic tracheal collapse which made breathing near impossible at times, Meemaw was expected to live mere days. And yet, Jill had made it her mission to make sure that those short days would not be spent in a shelter, that she be given a fighting chance to find happiness for however long..

Our transport queen, Jan Grissom, jumped in the car and broke land speed records to get to her. As she put her in the car to drive back to Georgia, she prayed that she would stay with her for the journey, so raspy was her breathing, so 'bone tired' from the lack of oxygen and at the end of the road she seemed.

As you know, we always give the dogs a celebrity name to go with their new family and new home. Meemaw, however, was so sick, and had seemingly so little time, that we decided not to change her name but instead have her keep the name as given by the Lee County team. It seemed so fitting, as she resembled everyone's vision of a kindly, caring old granny, full of love and compassion.

Our vet prescribed meds for her but cautioned about her lack of time and suggested we just make her comfortable for however long she had. So we set about 'bucket listing' her with the softest beds, more cuddles than should be legal and really, anything she wanted.

Soon, December gave way to January, and then all of a sudden we were in June pinching ourselves at our good fortune.

Meemaw, against all the odds, thrived and flourished at the cabins for almost 16 months, a miracle, to be certain. And what an amazing 16 months it was...every day a smile for whoever met her gaze, a reassuring nudge for whoever sat with her, and almost every day a near four digit-amputation for anyone who tried to feed her tidbits without using a flat palm.

She was a thing of beauty, a joy to behold every single day and I don't mind sharing that by last fall we had actually started to hope and believe she would actually live, and spread love, forever.

Last Friday, her heart said 'no more', and God whispered in her ear "It's time to come home, Poppet".

She took her last breath looking into the eyes of our team member Cindy, who said that she was relaxed, peaceful and knew that her work was done.

In our dreams, Heaven is populated by beings like Meemaw, who race, laughing, through fields of buttercups and daisies, where cloudless blue skies stretch to infinity, every breath is taken easily, there is no pain, and sausages and double bacon cheeseburgers are the size of skyscrapers and grow freely on hedgerows.

Meemaw, with her perfect temper and her gentle aura, gave us a glimpse of Heaven and proved beyond doubt that angels do

THANKS FOR STOPPING BY

exist. We just need to understand that sometimes they're a bit furrier than we expected.

God rest your beautiful soul Meemaw, and thank you for stopping by...

Rest In Peace.

FAREWELL TO LILY TOMLIN, THE FUNNY GIRL WHO TRIED TO SHANK US ALL...

MARCH 2021

Lily Tomlin has sadly left us...

She had been ill for some weeks, suddenly developing acute neck and back pain, didn't want to eat, she could barely even walk, it was painful for the FAAP team to experience.

Our veterinarians tried every trick in the book from steroids to cold laser therapy to acupuncture...she even stayed at the veterinary hospital for a week while they tried to figure it out and get the pain under control, but sadly nothing worked.

When she came home to us, in those last days before we

had to make this decision to let her go, she started circling to the right, which can be a sign of serious neurological issues... whatever it was, it was not good.

As a hospice care facility, our mission is not to prolong life.

Oh no, Ladies and Gentlemen, our mission is to provide excellent QUALITY of life, for as long as we can.

Once the animal is experiencing pain or misery that is untreatable, we won't ever keep them alive just for the sake of it.

Our decision to let Lily go was particularly sad because, first of all, she was the youngest dog we have ever had at the cabin. She was only 10 years old when she came to us, and 12 years old when she passed, after two years with us.

Secondly, Lily Tomlin represented unfinished business for so many of us.

You see, she spent a good deal of her day loving on her favorite people......and then the other half of it plotting ways in which she could kill the rest of us.

My normal eulogies for our senior babies are more romantic, I know, but honestly, I ain't gonna lie, Lily was a bit of a nightmare at times.

It's not that I didn't like her, quite the opposite in fact. I really admired her. She was ballsy as shit, in a 'lifer' female prison-inmate kind of a way.

Mmmm hmmmm....you just needed to look at that girl the wrong way, the whale eye would come out and you KNEW you could be headed for a 'Molly Whopping'.

If you ever watched Real Housewives of New Jersey and saw Teresa Giudice go at it with, well, anyone...yeah, that was Lily.

Beautiful, loving, kind and gentle...just as long as you didn't piss her off!

Okay, okay, I'm sorry, forgive me....I am, of course, taking artistic license to a whole new level here, but there is SOME truth to this and so we made allowances, worked with her and decided that she was a different kind of gift from God.

One to learn from...

You see, Lily had a rough life. Her and her 4 brothers and sisters were dumped at the shelter when the family just upped and left, the rest quickly got adopted, but Lily didn't show well during adoption events.

So, she batted her eyelashes and faked her passport to get into Frankie and Andy's Place, telling us she was 14. Stress really can make a dog look so much older.....and we bought it hook, line and sinker.

The cabin, with all of our loving human hands, was a lot for her though; woefully under socialized with people in her former life, but smart enough to know she needed them, Lily was drawn to other dogs for safety and friendship.

And that was okay.

We just let her work things out at her own pace, and were delighted with every small gain, every cuddle she allowed, every ear rub she would tolerate.

We allowed her to seek the care and security of the other dogs as much as she needed, instead of forcing human interactions on her (which NEVER goes well) and finally, were proud to see her become a nurturer/carer herself.

About 12 months in, she became somewhat of a hospice nurse for the seniors who were in their last weeks or months, guarding them from what she perceived to be inappropriate human touch, making sure they had room to eat, sleep and be left alone.

It was truly quite magnificent to watch her work....this little firecracker who would frantically make 'prison shivs' to stab those of us she didn't like (sensing a prison vibe much in this eulogy?), the girl who dreamed of mauling kind, dog-loving folks whose faces just didn't fit, turned out to be one of the kindest-hearted dogs we have ever had the fortune to meet.

Lily passed on the couch in the Big Dog cabin, her favorite spot in the world; her head in the lap of her Aunty Breanna who loved her fiercely, and whom she adored right back, as she slowly wilted off to sleep.

We couldn't heal her, and it killed us to know that, but at least we could give her the peaceful, quiet, loving send-off she wanted.

Lily is up there now, surrounded by our former cabin residents, playing with Boris, Sam Elliott, J-Lo, Tallulah Bankhead, Frannie....I can just envisage it now as they all ready themselves to meet us once again at the Rainbow Bridge.

I'll be asking God to 'frisk' Lily first though, to make sure she hasn't got a 'lock in a sock' or a sharpened toothbrush handle with a list of names written on the shank.....

Rest In Peace, sweet girl.

You were complicated, but such a beautiful soul...and you were loved.

Really, really loved.

And that's all that matters to us.

FAREWELL TO SNAZZY, WHO LIVED, LAUGHED AND LOVED...FIERCELY

MARCH 2022

Sometimes, it is hard for me write a eulogy.

Not because I don't know the dog or have no feelings for them.

Quite the opposite, in fact.

I have always found it hardest to write eulogies for my own dogs and the dogs that have impacted our lives in a very personal way, because writing, although cathartic, dredges up so many memories and thus, the pain of grief.

So it is with Snazzy.

Since Snazzy passed, there has not been not a minute since then that those of us close to her have not missed her terribly.

She was a Frankie and Andy's Place corner stone, and before that, a Desperate Dogs/ Miller family corner stone…and there will never be another dog like her.

We met Snazzy six years ago when a good friend of mine, Melissa, decided to foster a Brittany Spaniel to repay the joy that her own family of Brittany Spaniels had given her. Snazzy joined the Bosso household having lived her entire life up until then in a basement in Gainesville, able to roam on the family's land but with little to no human interaction. She lived down there, was fed, vetted, and that was it.

Better than some we see, it's true, but still a shameful life to force on a pack animal.

As with some good deeds, this one didn't go unpunished and the 'mild-mannered easy going dog' that Brittany Spaniel Rescue told Melissa she was going to be fostering, turned out to be a bit of a 'Bralligator' (Brittany spaniel/ alligator mix) at times, and nipped her pretty good in week two.

Melissa and her husband Dan knew that grandchildren would be on the way shortly, and so she asked me if we could help Snazzy, because she really didn't want to give up on her, but knew also that she couldn't keep her.

I agreed to do a behavioral consult and evaluate her at the Desperate Dogs Ranch, as long as Brittany Spaniel Rescue would let her first be examined by a veterinarian. So many dogs are castigated as 'aggression cases' when really they are just super painful, you see.

As was the case with Snazzy. This eleven year old girl had

arthritis so badly in her shoulders and elbows, that our veterinarian instantly put her on pain meds, anti-inflammatories and started laser therapy. She said to me that she didn't know how Snazzy had coped with the excruciating pain up until then.

And that was our first indication of this girls' indomitable spirit.

We were full with boarding guests on the day that Snazzy came to be evaluated for the weekend. My husband Pete looked at me and said "Jesus, Pen, you choose THIS weekend to evaluate her? A bite case?"

He soon shut up when I promised to make him a Yorkshire pudding (God, that man is so easily pleased!) and so we set about evaluating this pretty 11 year old girl, who walked tentatively like a cripple, because, well...she really was.

Over the weekend, we were so slammed, I didn't have as much time to work on her as I had intended, so I told the rescue, and Melissa, we'd keep her a few days into the next week and that she could leave us on the Wednesday when I had done multiple tests with multiple people.

We were careful with her, operated the usual minimal handling policy that we use with all bite cases, and she actually struck me as sweet and quirky, with a bit of a sense of humor almost poking through, which was a nice surprise. But I was absolutely not prepared for what I saw on the Wednesday morning, as she was due to go back to the rescue...it was something which changed everyone's lives.

Snazzy was in the side yard laying in the sun having just completed a half hour session with me. She'd done well and I was already mentally writing the report for the rescue, when all of a sudden, sweet little Sailor, a teeny tiny little 4 pound sassy pants who was boarding for the weekend, decided to jump on Snazzy's head and run all the way down her neck and jump off her tail. I knew Snazzy was dog friendly, but most dogs don't do stupid shit like Sailor just did and so I rushed over to stop anything before it escalated.

What happened next floored me.

Snazzy laughed.

Yes, she actually laughed! And then swatted her paw playfully at Sailor, rolled on her back and let Sailor jump back and forth over her body like an agility dog going through the poles.

And then came the deluge...ALL the little dogs in that group ran over to her and wagged their tails, play bowed; she swatted them playfully as they nuzzled her like a Mama.

She beamed.

She giggled.

She LOVED it!

When one of them became a bit too much, she gave a soft grumble and wiggled an eyebrow, and everyone was instantly contrite...until she invited them to clamber all over her again. And again. And again.

Oh, we knew then and there that we had something special, that this was a dog with a gift we could use.

Kathy Wick, one of our crew, came out to see what all the fuss was about and said to me "Well, I guess she ain't going anywhere then!" And winked.

And for the next two years, she didn't.

We adopted her to join the working pack at the Desperate Dogs Ranch and she made herself so useful, it was like she read the employee handbook, saw where there was a need and filled it.

Always ready to take care of the little guests, always ready to help out in a play session, Snazzy understood the assignment so well, even though it had never been explained to her.

I remember being off one day and, seeing that we had some gregarious dogs in, I asked Doug Dysart if he needed me to come in and help with the lunchtime Session. He laughed and said "It's okay, I've got Snazzy with me out there. No one's gonna take her on!"

In 2017, eighteen months after we opened Frankie and Andy's Place, our 'Head Girl', cabin matriarch Lil' Kim, died suddenly.

While we were all devastated at her loss, I was more worried at the gaping hole we had at the top of the pack. As a canine behaviorist of many years, I have seen many established dog packs fail after the death of an alpha figure; unable to cope without an ever-present calm, easy going but confident leader. Lil' Kim was some real hard shoes to fill.

I was out looking in the shelters and rescues for days and days on end, trying anywhere to find the right senior dog to replace her, but was just not finding the right personality to lead with calmness, strength and love. Then during our daily 'family time' coffee break one day, my husband Pete and team member Kathy both suggested Snazzy as Lil' Kim's replacement.

"She's got all the right credentials, she won't take any crap and she is EXACTLY the right personality to pull everyone together after their loss."

We tried her for an afternoon, then a day, then an overnight, and within a week, Snazzy was running the show up at the cabin like she was born to do so...it was perfection.

"Oi, Frannie! Take your tablets and quit playing with your food".

"No Boris, I don't fancy a shag, thank you very much...keep it in your pants, old man!"

"Naomi, stop playing hide and seek under the table".

"Victor, eat your vegetables or you'll not be able to poop, you know what you're like".

Everyone shaped up and straightened up at the presence of the new big-hearted Sheriff in town and once again, peace, calm and confidence reigned at the cabin.

But oh, how we missed her down at home and at the Desperate Dogs Ranch!

The Senior Dog cabin's gain was definitely our huge loss and even though we visited every day and brought her down to swim in our pool every week in the summer or to play with boarding guests on occasion so that she didn't feel she'd been fully rehomed, it was hard without her there.

Over time, her joints got worse and worse and her mobility became even more of an issue. Many is the time we thought we'd need to say goodbye, but each time she would rally and get back up.

I rarely knew a dog who loved her life as much as Snazzy, or who fought so hard to stay.

It was like she was saying "Listen guys, the first part of my life was pretty shit, I am going to ride this train for as long as I can now that I have it so good, and I ain't gettin' off without a fight".

We tried her with every medication, different Chinese herbs, every homeopathic, every supplement, and for a very long time, they worked beautifully. But of course, nothing lasts forever.

When Ranch Manager Kristen Snyder told me she felt like the time was coming, it wasn't because Snazzy was giving up, it was because her body finally was.

She was 17 years old.

Kris bought her cheeseburgers and yummy treats, gave her hot wraps every night and helped her into hot baths to ease her joints.

The care team had to use a sling to get her out to pee, and to keep her moving every few hours to prevent bed sores which was no small feat as, to be honest, home girl was a little bit of a heifer!

Her light didn't dim, her resolve never wavered though…and as long as she wanted to be there, our team moved heaven and earth to make her dream a reality. She was having a ball, right up until she wasn't.

On the day that Snazzy left us, she woke up and said "I'm all done now. I am ready to go and meet my maker. Let's go get this taken care of, Aunty Kris".

Kristen confided that she never saw a dog as ready, and who KNEW she was ready, and was so accepting of it. This alone is a gift for weary rescuers who, trust me, always second guess these final decisions.

For Snazzy to decree this, and make it so abundantly clear… well… it was just so Snazzy!

The girl was a legend.

From all of us who love you Snazzy… we just know you are up there, looking down, nit-picking about how we are doing things in your absence, wishing you were back in charge.

THANKS FOR STOPPING BY

This glorious old girl with her will of iron and heart of gold will live on in the cabin forever.

We were so lucky to know her, to learn from her, to enjoy her and to be amused by her.

Rest In Peace Snazzy girl, we will see you on the other side.

FAREWELL TO IAIN GLEN, OUR AMBER-EYED HEART-THROB

JULY 2021

We knew it was coming.

We prayed we could hold back the inevitable freight train of misery, prayed for a miracle.....but no.

It was not to be.

After months and months of ups and downs, good days, bad days, days where he was painful, days where he was super playful....finally Iain Glenn told us that it was time.

And we had to listen.

Those of you who know us well will know that there are cute

dogs, there are good looking dogs, there are even scrumptious dogs.

But then there was Iain. A dog set apart.

65 pounds of delicious caramel chocolate, with the most aristocratic nose and amber eyes that you could fall into...

Oh, and whiskers like a catfish, so that became his nickname. Pronounced by our staff and volunteers as 'CYATFISH' like we were all from the Bayou.

Oh man, Iain was a looker for sure...but it didn't stop there.

Iain was a dog that commanded your attention, made you fall madly in love with him but kept himself so infinitesimally out of reach, aloof in a kind of manly, Clint Eastwood-esque way, that you were never sure if you were his favorite or if he was secretly courting the charms of another.

He wasn't.

He just maintained an air of aloofness to underline his position as Head Honcho, unconcerned with the petty, small and inconsequential. He would give himself to you in the moment and then be on his way, but by then you were hooked, giddy with pleasure that he'd noticed you.

This is how he was with everyone but Parker Posy.

Parker, the 18 year old dainty husky with a whimsical and playful nature was his lady love, his best friend and his partner in crime.

We would be shocked and awed to watch Iain's madcap capers with his beloved Parker late at night, when we were trying to get all the dogs settled for sleep and the two of them were having a race around the dining table!

Parker was always too quick for him, but he was wily and as she flew around, he would nip in underneath and slip his body through the chairs so he could catch her 'on the fly'.

They often laid together, paws touching, like a little old couple in an assisted living facility, taking in each other's presence and basking in the glory of their love. Sharing unspoken jokes at the expense of the others half the time, I'm sure.

Iain's passing was not unexpected; we had made the decision to do surgery on the invasive cancer on his spine back in January, knowing that it would not save him, but hoping that it would give him time. He was a vital boy, he was beloved by humans and dogs alike......he was, after all, the cabin 'hottie'.

He came through surgery pretty well, all things considered, but the invasive tentacles of that monster on his spine were far reaching and hungry. We knew the cancer would rear its' ugly head again, it was just a question of when.

The surgery and the subsequent palliative treatments we opted for, did however buy him 6 months of peace, normality and pleasure.

He enjoyed his beloved Parker Posy, he still enjoyed his food, he loved a 'bimble' around the cabin grounds to check on security matters, his self-imposed duty. However, his favorite thing of all was to sleep on the porch outside the door of the Little Dog Cabin like The Guardian of the Gate, daring anyone to go past.

He was an absolute bloody nightmare to move when he was there, firmly ensconced on one of the padded outdoor beds, digging his heels in.

Many is the call we took down at the Desperate Dogs Ranch across the driveway from a volunteer trying to move him out of the blistering heat or the biting cold but who'd been told unceremoniously to 'bugger off' and leave him alone. That low grumble, top lip lifted in a sneer, amber eyes daring you to 'make his day'...yep, Clint Eastwood to a 'T'.

One of our staff would race up there, pop a slip leash on him, shove some warm chicken or steak in front of his face and he'd instantly perk up, soften his features and say 'Lead the way, Toots".

Those reading this might be tempted to think he was a bit of an asshole...nope, not at all. He just knew what he wanted and that was that.

He wasn't going to maul anyone to death, he was just the King of the grimace/veiled threat combo. And oh, how we loved him for it. It made us giggle.

On the day that he passed, there was no doubt that it was time.

He was losing his dignity along with his mobility and the constant toppling over and not being able to get himself up again was hurting his feelings way more than it hurt his body.

He had quite the gathering of people coming in to wish him well on the next leg of his journey...'swooning' volunteers, staff past and present, all of whom he graciously allowed to kiss him goodbye.

Doug Dysart, his favorite staff member and good friend for so long, whom he followed from cabin to cabin throughout every shift, came in to see him and kiss him goodbye...this was a tough one for Doug, but harder for those of us watching that sweet farewell.

Before he left his friend, Doug saw that Iain was embarrassed to have soiled himself and acted quickly to preserve his dignity, knowing it was all he had left. He calmly and quietly took him into one of the rooms and cleaned him up so that he would be all shiny and clean to meet his old pals Boris, Gerry and the rest of the gang whom he knew would be waiting for him in paradise. It was a kindness that was not lost on Iain.

His Aunty Cindy took him to the vets and, so that he wouldn't be scared, she insisted upon his ladylove, Parker, going with him. They sat in the car together all the way there, and then, when it was time, his girl Parker was beside him, letting him know to go on ahead and she'd see him on the other side.

Iain, you perfect, perfect boy, you broke our hearts. Why couldn't you just live forever?

This was such a tough one for all of us.

So long Cyatfish.

Rest In Peace, handsomest boy.

We'll see you on the other side....

FAREWELL TO PARKER POSEY, OUR PERFECT, SNOWY ENCHANTRESS

APRIL 2022

"One who possessed beauty without vanity,
Strength without insolence,
Courage without ferocity,
And all the virtues of man without his vices.
This praise, which would be unmeaning flattery if inscribed over human ashes, is but a just tribute to the memory of" Parker Posy, a dog.
(Adapted from Lord Byron's 'Epitaph to a Dog'. November 1808.)

Parker Posy, our perfect, petite Husky, left us last week, aged 20 years old or more, and the Frankie and Andy's Place family is still reeling from her loss.

She flitted and pranced her way into our lives in 2019, like a woodland nymph dancing through the trees....there, but just out of reach.

A firm favorite with Hickory Level Hound Rescue who needed to free up foster space so that they could save other lives on death row, when her foster mum brought her to the cabins, she cried at the thought of saying goodbye. While we sympathized with her emotion at that time, we had no clue as to the 'being hit by a Mack truck' quality of falling deeply in love with this girl and what it meant to a soul.

To know her was simply to be under her spell.

Despite her advanced years there was an eternal youth, an effervescence about her that was unquantifiable.

So light of foot and graceful of heart, it was as if a strong breeze would whisk her away, and yet a deeper footprint on these shady grounds is hard to imagine.

She loved deep...yet she laughed light.

She ate heartily at times...yet seemed to have no earthly need for food.

She feasted on relationships, particularly with her beloved Iain Glenn whom we lost last year...yet was somewhat of a loner.

She knew the power she had over others, she truly was a sentient being...yet she was the least self-aware dog we have ever met.

She brought everything to those she connected with, and yet there was always a feeling that she was keeping 'special things' locked inside.

She was the perfect greeter dog, enthusiastically welcoming every lost soul to the cabins, but oh, she was so much more than just 'front of house'.

Parker Posy was an enigma.

She was mesmerizing.

There will never, ever be another like her.

Parker Posy, thank you from the bottom of our hearts for the gifts you brought, for awakening our senses and for being a friend to every needy soul seeking refuge.

Rest In Peace, Angel, and we will see you on the other side.

FAREWELL TO ORVILLE REDENBACHER, WHO STOLE OUR HEARTS WITH HIS GOODBYE

APRIL 2023

Imagine a little black bear, cute as cute could be.

A shiny black nose like a glossy button that you just push for a dose of joy.

Fur so soft you could lose yourself in it.

Imagine a smile so bright and so wide that you could feel clouds parting in the sky to bring sunshine to the world, all because of its' very existence.

Imagine eyes literally dancing with mischief and enthusiasm, liquid pools of sunshine open and ready to greet each day, and each person, with love, warmth and welcome.

Ladies and gentlemen, welcome to the world of loving Orville Redenbacher.

Orville, the little Chow who popped into our lives unexpectedly, was the dog we didn't know we needed.

That is, until we met him…and then we couldn't live without him.

Orville was being fostered by our partner and co-founder, Penny Andrews, when we first met him. She had scooped him up hastily when his owners, whom she knew, had tried to have him put down due to his age and infirmity. They said he was at death's door and were on their way to the vets to euthanize him but Penny saw something there that was worth saving and said "I'm taking him with me now".

She immediately opened her home to him and was surprised when he settled so quickly and became instant great friends with her senior Chihuahua, JD. So much so, that she brought him to our sister organization across the driveway, The Desperate Dogs Boarding Ranch, to have a little vacation with JD while she travelled.

Immediately, this old boy came alive in the field, laughing and playing with everyone in the meadows at Desperate Dogs, always ready to 'pretend chase' the little ones like a kindly grandfather with a big 'GRRRRR" while laughing himself silly.

Orville was so warm and fuzzy, so human, we could not even believe our luck that we got to enjoy him. He was a gift.

Even more so, how he just seemed to have found his niche taking care of other dogs. Any new client dog, big or small, who was a little wary or nervous was partnered with Orville and he'd take care of them like a nanny.

When it came time for him to leave, we begged Penny if we could keep him with us and foster him at the Ranch; this new job, new sense of purpose, new diet and the rural environment was so obviously giving him a second shot at feeling good. He suffered from tracheal collapse which made him 'honk' on occasion but we had it under control with careful exposure to outside, controlled exercise and some non-traditional therapies.

We told her that he was right where he needed to be.

Thankfully, Penny agreed and so Orville settled in to the Ranch as a valued team member, working a little every day and getting more cuddles than any dog had a right to expect, just on account of his sheer gorgeousness…he really was pretty irresistible.

And then one day soon after, tragedy struck up at Frankie and Andy's Place.

Boris Karloff, our big, beautiful, kind, father figure, who oversaw the entire cabin pack, passed after a long time at the helm.

Quite apart from our grief, we wondered how we would manage without him. Boris' love, tenderness and kindly shoulder for any of the dogs in need was a huge factor in the balanced atmosphere of the cabins. The dogs all looked up to him and came to him with their emotional needs, which he happily fulfilled with a smile.

All dog packs need a leader, a gentle parental figure; someone in charge so that the others can relax and know things are being taken care of. No dog wants to have the responsibility for everything, especially if they are anxious.

Boris had been all those things and more, and the gaping hole he left was like a yawning chasm.

And that's when Orville rose like cream to the top.

We decided that in order to have the balance and ease that we needed to maintain at the senior dog sanctuary, perhaps Orville should be given a trial run at the top job?

From the first moment we opened the gate to show him his new home, he wagged and wiggled vociferously like he'd landed in a donut factory with a hall pass.

All the dogs came up to greet him and he immediately struck the perfect balance between humble newcomer and someone who could see the lay of the land and knew what needed to be done. It was literally awe inspiring.

"Hey, how are you? I'm new, can you show me where the water is?"

"Hi Toots, you sure do look fine, spot of dinner on the porch with me later maybe?"

"I see you, sweetie. I know, it's scary for me too, but come sit by me and we can be newbies together".

Oh. My. Word.

Never in our lives had we seen such a natural empathy; it came out of literally nowhere, and hit us like a tornado. He was all things to all dogs, a chameleon of personality, a gentler of spirits and an instant hit with the humans volunteering.

We brought him down to the Desperate Dogs Boarding Ranch every day for a few hours so he would still get a little taste of his old 'fairground' life while he transitioned but, all too soon, he was ready to stay at the cabins full time and assume his throne.

His new name, chosen by Doug Dysart, a pivotal, long-term figure in Cabin and Ranch life, was simply perfect as it combined the sweetness and saltiness of his personality. Orville could be hilarious, kind, but also kind of sassy and saucy. An incredible draw for anyone in his orbit as you were always guaranteed a giggle...and then some loving.

For three whole years, he reigned supreme; a perfect era in our short history, combining the wisdom of Solomon with the grace of Gandhi. Add to this his exceptional good looks when he wore his hair in a 'lion cut', there was not a man, woman or child who could resist him. In fact, we took him to schools more often than any other dog because his lion cut, with its' shaggy mane and close clipped body with a swish on the end of his tail made him look like Mufasa. That boy only had to enter a room and he would have all of the children giggling and smiling from the get-go.

In the summers, we got increasingly concerned with his breathing and, as the occasional honking and breathlessness got a little worse, we, along with our veterinarian, managed him more and more. But always in the cooler months he would bounce back like a rubber ball, eager to embrace the chill and the respiratory freedom it gave him.

Until last week.

Last week, his windpipe suddenly uttered its' last gasp. It said "Enough. I can't do this anymore, my old friend. I have served you well and to the best of my abilities for 16 years despite the harsh Georgia weather and now I am tired. I just cannot do another summer".

Cabin Manager Jen Calderhead took one look at him struggling to breathe that morning and raced him to the emergency vets. Despite receiving oxygen, he was fading, dying in front of her, and there was literally nothing that could be done to save him.

He passed very quickly in Jen's arms and although that is not the way any of us imagined his passing, we had hoped for more serenity in his final moments, Jen said the speed of it was both shocking and consolatory.

She kissed his beautiful face as the sedative eased his features, she told him how perfect he was, how the angels were all desperate to bring him into their hallowed ranks. Then she sank her fingers one last time into that luxurious inky black fur and breathed him in deep, to hold his scent inside her nostrils forever.

Orville left us knowing that he mattered, that his work and his life was valued. We know he found contentment in that.

Farewell old friend. May you rejoice in the songs of angels for eternity and greet all those who follow you with a smile and a warm touch, just as you did in life.

We adore you Orville Redenbacher, and always will.

FAREWELL TO TRISHA YEARWOOD, OUR BEAUTIFUL GOLDEN CHILD

SEPTEMBER 2022

Some things just aren't meant to be forever.

Take the beautiful Daylily for instance....it is an easy-going flower that does well in most soils, blossoms perfectly in full sunlight, when its' trumpets of vibrant color light up our lives and fill our hearts with awe at their beauty.

Sadly though, it blooms for just one day.

For some reason, that makes it even more special, even more perfect, doesn't it?

The lasting memory of the perfection we hold in our gaze,

even for just one brief second in time, is indelible proof of our good fortune that we beheld it at all.......

Such was our experience with the exotic and tender bloom that was Trisha Yearwood.

Trisha came into our lives, through Golden Retriever rescue of Atlanta, with the promise of 'today only'.

We knew that tomorrow was not, could not be, guaranteed.

A vile monster of a tumor lurked inside her beautiful head, gorging itself on her body, growing itself selfishly on her discomfort.

This sweet girl, only 11 years of age, seemed to know this too.

She joined the cabins with the unanimously shared express intentions of making the best of what little time she had, and, as if she had written her own manifesto, fell in love within minutes of walking through the doors. Arlene Jacobs, the sweet Frankie and Andy's Place volunteer who named her so perfectly, locked eyes with this golden beauty and from that moment on, there was not another person in the room.

Just as she had with her previous temporary foster mama, Trisha found a place to park her heart as she walked in, and didn't move from that spot. That girl was born to give and receive love. That was her entire purpose.

We had her for just 6 weeks.

Six weeks of battling to keep the monster inside her at bay, six weeks of daily fluids therapy, six weeks of cooking 10 different meal options a day to try to tempt her to eat, and of course, six weeks of realizing sometimes that only a McDonalds was going to hit the spot. Midnight runs to the "Big yellow M" became commonplace.

On the flip side, it was six weeks of soft eyes, a gentle paw placed on a knee saying "Please, just love me".

PENNY MILLER

Six weeks of perfect breath, enjoying the gentle rise and fall of her chest and knowing she was ours, like we had captured an angel.

Six weeks of watching her befriend every dog in her orbit, making them feel special, just as she did us.

Six weeks of watching her scratch up the dirt out in the yard and roll luxuriously in it, like she was reliving a misspent youth.

It wasn't enough, but to be honest, even a hundred years would not have been.

She was perfect, and thanks to Golden Retriever Rescue of Atlanta who entrusted us with her hospice care, she was our angel for 44 glorious days.

We knew it would be short.

We just had no clue it would be quite so vibrant, so glorious, so all-encompassing and so perfect.

And for that we are profoundly thankful.

Trisha Yearwood, thank you for stopping by on your journey.

We were honored to take care of a weary traveller, and even more honored, in the words of the great songstress Trisha Yearwood herself, 'to carry her home'.

Until next time, sweet angel.

FAREWELL TO BILL MURRAY, SUCH A SWEET AND GENTLE SOUL

SEPTEMBER 2023

Sometimes it's the quiet ones that leave the biggest space behind when they pass.

The ones who never ask for anything much.

The ones who are always grateful for every look, every touch, every kind word.

That was Bill Murray. A gentleman to his very last breath and a sweeter soul you'd be hard pressed to meet.

Bill came to us almost two years ago via our friends at

PENNY MILLER

Forsyth County Animal Shelter, where he had gone after having been found stray.

He was chipped, so the owner was located but absolutely refused to come for him. Kathy at the shelter called me and said "I have the perfect dog for Frankie and Andy's Place. He is amazing, but the Douche Canoe who owns him, doesn't want him, clearly".

Ugh...We have known many jerks in our 8 years of Frankie and Andy's place but the total idiot who let this angel go just about tops the list.

His soft brown eyes, his gentle manner, his endearing shuffle...this boy had it all in spades.

As we always say, 'One man's trash is another man's treasure'.

Oh, and what a treasure he was.

Bill entered the cabin like a whisper on the wind, easing himself into the group with no fanfare, no fuss, just a polite "Hey, I'm Bill, happy to be here".

We love dogs like him as they are always responsible for maintaining the calm, zen-like atmosphere of the cabins. Bill always laid in a cool spot, out of the way behind the couch, and the only thing he ever demanded was his food, on time, and plenty of it, thanks very much.

His mobility was poor, as is often the way with all of our incoming dogs, but he valiantly stood up and shuffled around to take care of his business. He did this right to the very end, even when every step was agony. That was just sweet Bill's way, never wanting to be a problem for another, preferring to do it himself if he could.

Bill was a tactile soul who craved touch and trust me, our amazing volunteers never left him wanting.

He was massaged every day, he was brushed every day and he got warm wraps on his hind limbs on the days that the damp rain or heat and humidity went to his legs. He would sigh with a deep, deep sound that welled up from his stomach almost... content and happy to be touched, to be noticed and to know that he mattered.

The anti-inflammatories, both natural and prescription, the pain meds, the glucosamine, warm wraps, massage, light treatments....when they all failed him, we knew it was time.

Bill would have carried on forever, though, struggling to put one foot in front of the other, wincing and stumbling with every step.

His mind was good, perfect even; his body had failed him, though.

Even though the indignity of incontinence bothered him so greatly, still he wanted to be here to please us all, to take care of us, to keep his title as Head Chocolate Lover Boy.

These are the times when to let a beautiful soul go is hard, as you all know.

But we are all, and only, about quality of life for our beloved residents. Once that is gone, and pain is intolerable and unfixable, then it is time.

His Aunty Jen took him to the vets where she laid on the floor with him, kissing him and nuzzling him as he slipped away gently.

Our oath to these beautiful souls is that none shall pass without being in the arms of someone they love, not one.

They all die in our arms, no matter the circumstance.

They are always offered a little chocolate just before the needle goes in, because at that point it really won't matter, but oh, such a delicious way to go...

Their passing is always gentle and slow, and always tender.

It is the greatest final gift we can give them, and we insist on it because there is not one among us who would want to die any other way.

So now the cabin is without our beautiful chocolate boy and, while the work load may be a little lighter, and the daily clean up a little easier, there is not one of us who wouldn't turn the clock back in a heartbeat for one more kiss, one more outstretched paw.

Rest in peace Bill Murray.

Kiss Patti, Harrison, Boris and the gang for us.

Thank you so, so much for being here.

FAREWELL TO PATTI LABELLE, THE HAPPIEST DOG IN THE WORLD

JULY 2023

Our little fighter, 'Patti the Magnificent', sadly lost her battle last week.

Despite the best efforts of so many, from our veterinarians to our donors, staff and some very caring volunteers, this sweet and most perfect of souls is gone.

Every loss is huge to us all, as no dog is more important than any other, but somehow there is a more defined sense of loss with Patti because we all felt...no, we KNEW...she would survive.

She was doing so well, how could this happen?

Even that very morning of her death, she was up and about, wagging her tail and eating her breakfast. The staff text loop was full of admiration for how she had bounced back from her last blood transfusion and how it had given her a completely new lease of life so quickly after she had been flagging a bit.

Immune-mediated hemolytic anemia is a terrible disease that creeps up and keeps creeping up over time, requiring drugs for life and in Patti's case, blood transfusions, to keep her steady. She was responding well to the treatment one moment...until she wasn't the next, it seems.

And that, dear friends, was the heartbreaker.

Her passing was such a shock we are all still getting over it; even today, we still trying to process it.

What remains is the knowledge that, thanks to you all and your generosity, we were able to throw every single possible treatment at Patti, give her the very best of care to recuperate, and give her the love and support she needed.

Patti enjoyed her life immensely, and in all honestly, how could she not?

She only had to flutter those eyelashes and someone would swoop in to pick her up.

She only had to wiggle that butt to get a scratch and an 'oooh' or an 'ahhh' from any human lucky enough to be in her orbit.

She had perfected the 'shabby chic' hairdo to such a level that many of us were wondering how we could achieve the same look...to the shock of a few local hairdressers.

She was kind to a fault. Her gentle grace brought something

to the cabins unseen since the legendary Carol Burnett, our original 'therapy dog for therapy dogs'.

Cozying up to this one, always stopping for a chat with that one, helping Cabin Mama Chrissie Hynde maintain the balance of calm and support in the cabins, this girl was everyone's friend.

Patrick Dempsey, the little Yorkie who struggles due to his lack of sight, depended on her companionship in his bed during a storm, and her warm body next to his on a cold night.

Jay Leno, our ailing Italian greyhound, has been thrown into crisis by her loss....she was his friend and confidante, and he has needed extra attention this week as the grief has affected him so physically.

While to hear of this is no doubt painful, we do try to turn grief on its' head and think of it as a positive. For remember, dear friends, these are the dogs that have been cast aside, dumped like trash, they are the dogs that no one cared about.

Found wandering stray, tied up to posts, left in empty homes with no food or water, these dogs were the forgotten that didn't matter to those family members tasked with their care.

In their last chapter, here at Frankie and Andy's Place, they matter so much that we reel from their loss and feel it like a physical ache.

Yes, it's truly painful, but what a fitting emotion and legacy for such perfect creatures. Finally, and rightfully, they are important, they have a purpose, their lives have value.

Patti Labelle, you were a magnificent sunbeam, drenching us in God's perfect light.

You were an integral part of our story and we will never, ever forget what you brought to us, the gifts you gave.

PENNY MILLER

For you mattered, sweet girl.....oh, how you mattered.

Thank you to all of you who helped with her care, for you truly prolonged and improved her life.

It is down to you all that we were able to keep her with us as long as we did.

Nighty night little Princess, Rest In Peace.

FAREWELL TO MERYL STREEP, A BALLSIER BROAD WE NEVER KNEW...

NOVEMBER 2022

In the list of hardest-to-write eulogies ever, this one ranks among the top five.

How do you encapsulate in words something, someone, so massive, so important, so fierce...and yet so small?

To try to do Meryl Streep justice is akin to trying to pushing back the tide of the ocean.

I suggest you take a moment to read the tale of Celtic Queen Boudicca, whose passions and strength truly embody the term 'fire and ice', to get even a tiny semblance of an idea as to who this little Rat Terrier/ Chihuahua mix was.

A more determined dog (but oh, SO much more than a dog) we never knew.

This tiny, bird-like creature arrived at Frankie and Andy's Place from Peach County Animal Shelter where her champion, Beth Moote, had campaigned for a few weeks for us to take her, bombarding me with videos and texts.

"She is perfect for you all, she needs you for sure but she is so special, you actually need her there too…just wait til you meet her!"

At that time we were full to the brim and so we asked Beth if they could wait a while?

Well, as is a regular fact of our mission, we pretty soon lost a special soul, and so straight away invited Beth to bring her up to us so we could see if she would work out at the sanctuary.

In she strutted, like John Travolta in 'Saturday Night Fever', a whopping 18 years old, legs like she was walking on stilts… this fiery old bird (she kind of looked like a blue heron in miniature) picked her way around the yard with an authoritative air that said "I've arrived. Have your people get my bags sent up to my room and unpacked, I'll be taking the woodland view suite".

Well, as you all know, there is nothing we like more than a frisky, self-opinionated, personality-laden dog. They make the world go round don't they?

So that was a firm yes from us!

At first, we treated her with kid gloves, until pretty soon we realized it was actually HER treating US with kid gloves and as the real Meryl Streep unfolded, so did the toughness and chutzpah of Estelle Getty.

We didn't even know what hit us!

Barking instructions, rounding up the other dogs like her own personal herd of sheepdogs, she was even performing security checks morning, noon and night on the perimeter fence. Always demanding this or that as the dogs' self-appointed union representative, Meryl worked hard every moment of the day for herself, for the cabins and for her friends.

"Get that dinner on the stove now! Justin Timberlake looks like he's starving hungry!"

"Sir Anthony needs a pee! Hellloooooo? Anyone?"

"If Otis Redding doesn't stop trying to shag me, Imma smack him in the face!"

And then just days later, both conversely and perversely, "Otis, wanna come sniff my goodies? Looks like I'm coming into heat!"

Dear Lord, it was a rollercoaster ride of laughs, indrawn breaths, shaking of our heads, giggles and 'Ahhh' moments.

Then, one day, without a whiff of warning, her eyes started to swell up, a lot. Despite our best efforts, the swathe of medications we threw at the problem didn't help. Surgery was the only option to stop the pain, which was hellish for her.

"This is it", we thought, "She won't survive the massive surgery to remove her eyes, she's too old". In truth, we hadn't even spayed her because of the risk of major surgery at her age, so how would she fare?

But the pain she was in and the thought of NOT taking the chance on her was unbearable and so we went ahead and had her eyes removed.

She survived the surgery well enough but developed a

roaring infection in her empty sockets a week afterwards and, scared to death, yet again we asked ourselves, would she survive?

Three weeks after the surgery, after multiple visits from the wonderful vet who made house calls to tend to her at the cabin, as well as us doing twice daily treatments with Chlorhexidine and Manuka Honey, she turned the corner and that's when we started to exhale a little.

A few months after her surgery we found that she was, if anything, even more confident than before, picking her way around the yard with the prowess of a cat. It was nigh on impossible to tell that she had no eyes; Meryl's other senses had kicked in, and they were ready for action!

Back in March of this year, at the age of 20, Meryl developed an awful UTI and it was then that we found her kidneys were not functioning well. We felt it may be the end, and prepared ourselves for it, while determining that we would do anything we could to help her, but only for as long she wanted us to.

We knew her well enough to know that she would let us know exactly what she was thinking.

She rallied well and a week later was back to her old self, although a little slower and a little less feisty but still with so much verve it was shocking.

Three months ago, another UTI and this time a new vet, hired days before and fresh out of school. The young man, who didn't know her at all, did a very quick examination and told us with great pomposity that we should let her go because of 'quality of life issues'. This pronouncement was made with no knowledge of the dog, her lifestyle, what her normal was...he just looked at her blood work and saw a high white blood cell count combined with the words '20 years old'.

Of course we felt that we were far better placed to make such decisions than someone who had seen her in an unnatural environment for less than five minutes, so we told that fool to stuff his unqualified opinions where the sun doesn't shine and insisted we would wait and see.

Thank God we did.

Even with failing kidneys and heart issues, she rallied again and was soon back to eating up a storm and marching around the cabin, schmoozing with Busta Rhymes and the gang, like all was well.

At that point, because we were in hospice care mode with her, Ranch Manager Aunty Kristen was doing a thrice weekly run to get her favorite cheeseburgers, she was getting weekly massages from her Aunty Marilyn, occasional car rides from her Aunty Pat and had more visitors coming to see her than a Head of State.

She loved the attention, drank in the fuss and got spurred on by it all.

Until last week, when she finally pronounced that enough was enough.

At 21 years of age, she looked around and said "Yep, I'm done."

She was still eating, still barking up a storm, and yes, she was still having some good moments, but the moments of pain and discomfort had become greater and it was clear she could not settle without difficulty.

The night before she left us, it took hours to make her comfortable enough to sleep, despite her medications and the use of CBD and massage, warm water wraps etc.

We had to call it.

PENNY MILLER

Her Aunty Jen bundled her up close to her chest, where she had spent a good many of her hours at the cabin, and drove her to the emergency vets where Meryl let them know exactly what she thought of them the minute they started poking her about.

Our Meryl, fully 'large and in charge' right to the end, went out with more of a bang than a whisper.

Thank you God for the life of Meryl Streep and the amazing time we had with her.

Thank you Peach County Animal Shelter for insisting she was perfect for us. You were right.

Thank you to all of you at home who loved her and supported her care with your donations.

And thank you Meryl for everything you brought to Frankie and Andy's Place.

You are unforgettable.

FAREWELL TO LIL KIM, FIRST LADY OF FRANKIE AND ANDY'S PLACE

SEPTEMBER 2017

The Queen is dead. Long live the Queen!

Today, sometime before two pm, our darling cabin matriarch, Lil Kim, passed away in her sleep.

She spent the morning enjoying her time outside with volunteer Shannon Davis playing with Boris and the gang, and generally revelling, as she did every day, in cabin life.

Shannon left the cabin at midday, and when Amie, our afternoon volunteer, came in at 2pm, Lil Kim appeared to be sleeping deeply. Amie tried to wake her up and only then realized that she would not be opening those amber eyes ever again.....

For those of you who never met this special girl, I can only begin to tell you what an incredible creature she was.

Found for us at Gwinnett Animal Control in May 2016 by a friend of Frankie and Andy's Place who had gone to the shelter that day to look at another dog for us, Lil Kim wasn't even on our radar. Sadly, the dog that the lady went to check out was not a fit for us, but she turned around and saw this beautiful slate grey beauty with amber eyes looking at her as if to say 'Me! Look at me! I am just what you are looking for....!'

And boy, was she right!

Lil Kim was the first ever cabin dog, and a real trail blazer!

She let us know very quickly that she did not want us to take our time filling the place with needy dogs, and insisted we get the ball rolling even quicker than we had planned. As they came in, one by one, first blind Trudy, then Amy, then Boris, then Cody, then Donald, Lil Kim was at the door to greet them all and show them the ropes....

'Don't poop there, Cody!'

'Leave his bowl alone until he's finished, please, Amy..'

'No humping allowed, Boris!'

'Donald, you're too short to try and climb on the table during dinner service, grow up you old fool!'

Little by little, she took these old no-hopers, fresh from the shelter, dumped by their loved ones, scarred with disease and a widescale dashing of dreams, and instituted a framework of family, a sense of belonging and a feeling that there was a parental figure at the cabin full time, around the clock.

They all flocked to her side whenever she beckoned them,

gave her a wide berth when she demanded it, and no one EVER second-guessed her.

As our beloved hospice care dogs Cody and Donald grew weaker and weaker, Kim looked out for them, and let us humans know it was almost time, and that we must be prepared....

When they passed, she sat like Mufasa the Lion King on the rock, just feet away from her beloved friends, kindly watching every move but still maintaining her distance...and her dignity.

Every thought, every action was grace personified.

It was as though she was here to teach us how to set this thing up, how to pick the dogs [she temperament tested every single dog that came to the cabin], how to grow our numbers carefully but steadily, and how to maintain a familial closeness, no matter what was going on outside or inside.

'Tornado warning? It's okay everyone, follow me and Aunty Pen down to the Ranch....Boris, you take a group with Aunty Linda. Errol Flynn? Quit messing around and get in the van before this rain carries us off!'

Life with her was a lesson in military leadership....precise, decisive, effective and yet always benevolent. A true pack leader.

As the numbers grew and grew to over 10 dogs, she revelled in her position and ruled even more beautifully over her domain, with her husband of choice, Pit/ Sharpei/ Boxer mix Boris Karloff.

Every day the two of them would walk out into the yard and survey their homelands, check on their charges, and start the ritual of cleaning, cleaning, cleaning. Kim cleaned him incessantly, wagging her tail with joy at being able to minister to her man.

Boris, being a bit of an old rascal enjoyed her spousal

ministrations but would always have a wink and raised eyebrow for the lovely Fiona, a saucy Beagle, when Kim wasn't watching! We truly suspect Boris is French, needing to have a wife AND a mistress!

Lil Kim was named after my own departed sister Kim, in whose honor we started rescuing senior dogs, and stumbled upon the most amazing way to spend a life you can ever imagine.

My sister was a sweet, sweet soul whose life ended too soon, but whose legacy of grace lives on in every dog we rescue, but none more so than Lil Kim.

Why 'Lil' Kim? Well, I wanted to name her after my sister but I am not fond of one syllable names for dogs, plus this gorgeous canine was a dark girl with one hell of a big beautiful booty...just like rapper Lil Kim! So Lil Kim it was.

Lil Kim died in exactly the way she would have wanted to, and is our first dog to die unassisted at home, of natural causes.

The enormous benign tumor that wrapped around her chest and armpit pressed on her heart and lungs crowding out internal organs. And then of course, there was the huge cancerous tumor on her back end which was a ticking time bomb. We will never know which struck the blow, but we are grateful to know that it was fast and that she died in her sleep.

She was found in a relaxed sleeping position, in her favorite spot, looking as graceful and peaceful as a soul ever did. A truly beautiful way to go, it was so like our Kim...on her own terms, in her own time, with no muss and no fuss.

I don't know what the first 12 years of this dear girls' life were, and how she got to be a stray, I always wondered if someone was looking for her. I could never understand such a pearl being cast aside. I know that in the early days, there was at times a sadness about her that could not be lifted, as if she missed her person, then she would shake off her melancholy and move on.

What I know for sure is that, for the last 18 months since coming to the cabin, this girl knew only love, only a gentle touch, only soft words.

Every day was a joy for her, every visitor was a friend and every single one of her family, both human and canine, doted on her.

She needed to be important to someone.

She needed to be responsible for someone, it's just who she was. In the last 18 months, she knew she mattered.

Kim, my darling, you were beloved by all of us. Your grace, your heart, your courage and your spirit will live on in every single loving moment up at that cabin.

Thank you, my sweet, for showing us the way.

Nighty night. X

FAREWELL TO BORIS KARLOFF, FIRST GENTLEMAN OF FRANKIE AND ANDY'S PLACE

FEBRUARY 2020

It really wasn't a case of 'You had me at Hello'.

He walked towards me and my friend Eileen, two mature chicks 'out on the pull' on a lovely sunny day in June 2016, and to be honest, we'd seen far better looking males in our time.

Skin all scabby, bad breath...no, make that HORRIFIC breath, plus, he walked like he'd been 'knobbled' by Misery Chastain.

Then of course, there was 'The Testicle'.

An entire planetary being all of its own, I'd never seen anything quite like it.

Eileen was speechless.

We were looking at each other, and then back at him, then quizzically back at each other, trying to fathom out that massive 'appendage' and also trying to decide at the same time if we should pick him, and anoint him as the luckiest guy in the world to be coming home with us.

In the end, it was that shy smile, that silent plea, that world of pain behind a tiny ray of sunlight in his eyes.

There was a kindness about him, a sense of justice......I'm sure it's going to sound stupid but he honestly looked, even then, like the kind of guy who'd help a damsel in distress.

And that, my friends, is how volunteer Eileen Cargell and I picked Boris Karloff to be the 4th of the original Frankie and Andy's Place dogs to come and live at the cabin.

Oh yes, sorry, I completely forgot to say that I was talking about a dog and not a fella!!

In many ways, everything seemed wrong; he was a melange of boxer, Pitt bull, Shar-Pei, and a few other incongruous breeds that were just hanging around that day on the shelf.....and yet somehow, it all just worked, like the most perfect jigsaw ever.

We said yes.

Of course we did.

The next day, my husband Pete picked him up to take him to the vets for his health screening.

The news was not good.....

Cancer of the prostate, a heart murmur of 6/6, serious

malnutrition following years of neglect, double ear infections, mange, and allergies had caused massive infected skin sores. To add insult to injury, most of his teeth needed to come out, but we couldn't put him under to fix them because of his heart murmur.

Ugh, it was a veritable disaster.

"Two months, maybe three" said the vet.

He was so weak, he needed so much care; footbaths, ear-washes, shampooing twice a week, medications out the wazoo, a special home-cooked diet rich in antioxidants to help heal his body and try to prolong his life…Oh dear God, it was such a lot.

"Are you guys up for this?" the vet asked as she listed his needs.

"Well, let's just see what we can do for him, and give him as good of a time for as long as we can, eh?" was our decision.

We took him home and that's when the fun started.

He may have been dying of all kinds of problems with his 'wedding tackle', but that didn't mean he didn't want to keep using it!

You could see him lasciviously eyeing up Lil Kim, the cabin matriarch, from morning til' night, planning how he was going to have his wicked way. He could barely walk, but it didn't stop him! He would amble over, pelvis pulsating like a jackhammer and she would tell him in no uncertain terms that she was FAR too much of a lady for any of that nonsense. The stony glare, the whale eye and the magnificent deep grumble she would erupt with would quell even the strongest 'uprising'.

Didn't stop him from eyeing her up like a freshly baked cinnamon roll, though……

And boy, when food was around, he was a bloody nightmare!

Thankfully, we knew what to expect with dogs that had been starved; they never really trust that food will be plentiful for ever even though everything about their life is now different, so we slowly built his trust with multiple daily smaller meals fed from our hands, and crated him when everyone else was eating, to stop him from being the playground thug stealing everyone's packed lunch!

Three months came and went before we even realized, then four months, five months......

We soon lost a beautiful soul called Cody, a massive Rottweiler with a gentle heart who had come to us for end of life care and this was truly the turning point...

Boris was feeling a little better by now and it was as if he realized it was his turn to step up.

As time passed, so this shift gradually took place......our tiniest dogs (startlingly for us) were to be found first thing in the morning nestled in the warmth of his ever increasing belly, him purring away at their trust in him. And as their trust in him grew, so did his benevolent nature.

Errol Flynn, the very first chihuahua we took in, would go to him for play, for snuggles, for adventure, or even just to sit beside him for company.

Boris' door was always open. They became the best of friends and it was his easy way with Errol that gave us all the confidence to let this happen organically.

Naomi Watts, a teeny weeny little chihuahua with a real sergeant major attitude, used to see Boris as her big brother, always ready for a few naughty pranks with her, or to get her out of trouble if she'd pushed her luck, which was pretty much every day. One high pitched Diva squeal aimed at her cabin mates, and

Boris would come awkwardly bimbling along with his trademark 'just spent twenty years on a horse' gait and would ask, "What's up, sugar cakes? Do I need to look sternly at someone?"

Ha! Sternly? What a joke!

He'd try but never quite pull it off, everyone knew he was a pushover.

Gilda Radner thought he was the bees knees and used to traipse around the cabin all day and night trying to be closer to him. A close and deep personal friendship developed between these two that would survive disabilities, surgeries, neurological issues, so many kinds of trauma......he was her man and she adored him. When Gilda had her eye removed, we worried about her state of mind coming back to the cabin with her vestibular disease and now dealing with only one eye.

Boris took care of it.

Just by being there for her.

When Naomi Watts was failing and the vets sent her home to enjoy her last days in peace at home, we stopped all meds because she hated them so much and instead put her in the hands of her beloved big brother.

Nestled in his loving paws, she not only restored, but thrived, better than ever, full of piss and vinegar and all because of that soft, loving nature. It was all she needed.

It was all any of us needed.

His darling 'second wife', saucy Beagle Fiona, whom he fell deeply in love with after the death of Lil Kim, was the victim of a very nasty dog attack, and was emotionally scarred. She found her joy again after returning home from a lengthy vet hospital stay, in the company of her man, whose winsome smile and affable nature turned her life around, made her feel safe, protected, and eventually comfortable living with all of the other dogs again.

Three pound Ilsa, whose poor little broken body had all the elasticity of a dry twig, went to Boris for love, protection and fun. It was nothing short of incongruous to see this teeny, tiny body clambering all over him as he slept. We would gasp as we would find her perched on top of his big old head, running over there to pick her up and inwardly screaming "Noooooooooooooooo!"

But, he never snapped, never said a word, never even made One. Wrong. Move.

It was as if he was frightened that his very slightest indrawn breath would stop the perfect moment, destroy her perfect trust in his acquiescence.

So many people counselled me to separate the big dogs from the littles, told me we were asking for trouble and yes, yes, I have to say that there was one time that it was not the best decision. But with Boris, had I tried to keep him away from the tiny cabin family members he had taken a blood oath to protect, it would have been mutiny.

Every single man, woman, dog and child who visited the cabin knew that it was right, knew that he was the righteous and bountiful father figure we needed in there so badly. He was Aslan, Gideon, Atticus Finch, all rolled into one.

Our veterinarians routinely suggested letting Boris 'work his magic' with sick dogs at the cabins, they had seen it so often, and knew his power.

His healing magic never, ever failed.

Every single dog that comes to us has a horrific tale to tell.

Boris' own tale was most unsettling, discovered by Animal

PENNY MILLER

Control hobbling down Kilcrease road in Barrow County in the scorching hot, unforgiving, Georgia sun, his battered and depleted 15 year-old body struggling to move on the hot asphalt, but oh so desperate to get away from the hell hole whence he came. The dents of an embedded collar and patches of bare leathery skin that could have been caused by scalding or chemicals there for the gasping.

When helping his cabin brothers and sisters, he himself had walked a thousand miles in those shoes and saw it as his sworn duty to help make their lives better.

A truly empathic soul.

Such a huge job.

Such a massive heart.

For three and a half years he fathered every lost soul, nurtured every world-weary human and created an oasis of love and calm in the middle of this small Georgia woodland.

Because of his love, and out of his kindness, we grew.

Because we could see, right in front of us, what could be achieved with a dog like him, with a heart like his, that's how we have exceeded all expectations.

You see, we were only ever going to measure our success in the number of happy dogs we created and the pleasure level of the humans who were touched and then healed by them.

Boris saw what we were trying to do…then lit a candle to show us the way.

As a younger woman I used to watch that show 'Touched by an Angel', and wished with all my heart that a beautiful angel would come and visit, and make everything okay.

Three and a half years ago, my dream came true.

Our collective dream came true.

While I am sobbing as I write this tribute to him, my heart swells with pride and gratitude that we got to experience this enormous love, this unfathomable depth of caring.

It was, honestly, life changing.

He really was all these things and more, we are so much the poorer for his passing.

Nighty night you big gorgeous boy...sleep well and rest easy.

You were simply magnificent.

FAREWELL TO FRANKIE, GODFATHER OF THE MISSION, AND THE ONE WHO STARTED IT ALL...

OCTOBER 2017

One look.

That's all it took.

A pair of huge liquid eyes, an indignant but huge, soft mouth and combover ears so crazy that they made his face a study in imperfect perfection.

I arrived at the Northeast Georgia shelter to volunteer that afternoon over ten years ago, not knowing that I was going to meet someone who was going to change my life forever.

But I did, and that someone was Frankie.

A huge Great Dane but oh, he was so skinny.

His owners had left him a month earlier, tied to a post in their backyard with no food or water for days (a common story here in Georgia that we rescuers deal with all the time). Fortunately, and unfortunately for him though, he had been rescued and ended up the shelter, where he had been treated for a severe lung infection. The unfortunate bit is that he had then been fostered out to someone who kept him in an outside pen, because they were frightened of what he would do to their cat. He'd been returned as he was not flourishing, the infection kept coming back, and so he was sadly hurtling towards his 'exit date'.

Then he locked eyes with me, and it was love at first sight, instant fireworks.

All the way home, he had his head on my shoulder as I drove, looking at me in the rear view mirror, eyes telling me that I would not regret this hasty move. We had just moved into a new house, had three big dogs already, and needed another one like a fish needs a bicycle, but what can I tell you? The heart wants what it wants...

Over the next three weeks our lives were turned upside down, he climbed up on top of the fridge to get at a bag of grapes and a whole catering size jar of peanut butter which he demolished entirely in the twenty minutes I was out sweeping the driveway. I rushed him to the animal hospital where the vet had him under observation all day, looked at me and said "Penny, welcome to the world of Great Dane ownership...if you put it on top of the fridge then OF COURSE he's going to find a way to get it!"

He was needy, he was loud, he was funny, he was famished, he was huge…and he was absolutely downright fascinating. I couldn't get enough of him.

Unfortunately, my oldest boy, our middle aged Weimaraner Nelson didn't feel the same way, and set about making Frankie's life a misery at every opportunity, to the point where we had to keep them apart, permanently.

Nelson's heart did not want what mine wanted, obviously.

So, three weeks after he left the shelter, Frankie was moved into our unfinished basement. My son Joe selflessly moved down there with him and braved the lack of heat and air for months on end so that Frankie would never be lonely. Together we set about building up his health, working on some of his issues and helping him to trust humans again, all the while looking for the perfect forever home where he could have it all.

Well, in the end, we did so much more than that, we found him his very own Penny. One with movie star looks and a heart as big as the moon.

Owner of a beautiful female Great Dane, Milan, Penny Andrews had convinced her then-boyfriend to meet Frankie so that they could have dogs that would be friends.

Penny took one look at him, her heart melted and she knew he was her soul mate. Even though he was ostensibly supposed to be her boyfriend's dog, she had always wanted Frankie for herself, and when they split up, the loss of him from her life was devastating. When the boyfriend turned out to be a bit of a douchebag and wasn't treating Frankie right, leaving him alone in the house for 14 hour stretches, I immediately drove down to get him back, angry that this dog was yet again not having the love and life he deserved. On the way to get him I got a call from Penny, in floods of tears.

"I need Frankie" She said.

"But Penny" I told her, "You live in a small condominium, how will you manage with two Great Danes in a small space?"

And then she said the words that tied me to her forever…"Let him come to me and I will buy him a house with a yard".

Two months later, she delivered on her promise, and all three of them, her, Milan and Frankie, moved into a fabulous home in Brookhaven.

Thus became the way of things…Frankie wanted, or Frankie needed, so Frankie got.

Now don't get me wrong, this did not in any way turn him into a brat, he just had a sense of his own worth unlike any dog I have ever known. He had a presence that drew people and dogs to him like bees to a honeypot, and he knew it instinctively, so he worked it.

Unashamedly.

Over the years, Penny and I became closer and closer, and decided, when we saw the need for it, that we would open a senior dog shelter together one day. As Milan passed and then Frankie grew older, the way forward was shown very clearly to us by the dogs, who told how, when and where it must happen.

Along with Penny's sister, Krystle, whose own dog Andy was a special senior visitor to the Ranch, we opened Frankie and Andy's Place in April 2016. Sadly, the sweet, gentle Andy died a week before the cabin was delivered, and now rests right by the entranceway in front of the Little cabin. However, Frankie was there on delivery day, directing the cabin placement operation, barking instructions, making sure everyone did their bit to make it perfect.

He was the motivation behind Frankie and Andy's Place, the driving force behind our unique senior dog sanctuary. Without him, and his mum who saw it all so clearly…it would not exist.

On Tuesday Frankie left us.

He had degenerative myelopathy and had not been able to move himself for a few weeks; when it was clear he could not get better from this, his mum made the decision to have a last perfect weekend with him, and then say goodbye in a way befitting his rank and dignity.

His final needs were taken care of in the beautiful meadow down at his second home, the Desperate Dogs Ranch, by his friends at Gwinnett Animal Hospital and Frankie slipped away peacefully surrounded by those of us who loved him, looking deep into the eyes of the love of his life, Penny, Andrews, their gazes locked for eternity.

I needed to share with you this story, about how he came to be so very fundamental to our very existence, but what I really want is to share these next words, and to let them rest on your hearts. Penny Andrews spoke these words to him just before he passed and it was beyond beautiful……

"Right now I struggle with two thoughts….why does he have to go? And, why me?

I don't know why I was so blessed in getting Frankie, but I know I was.

It was like my lot in life was a combination of caring for Jesus and a supermodel mashed together; a Diva and a Deity.

In one sense he pushed me beyond anything I ever thought

possible; he opened my mind to see things I had never seen before he came along.

We all have teachers in life.....people that mould us and make us reach for the stars, people who see more in us than we think is possible. Mine came in a furry body, with a loud bark and floppy combover ears. I don't know why I was gifted, but I know I am so much better, so much stronger because of him.

John Keats said 'I almost wish we were butterflies and liv'd but three summer days-

Three such days wth you I could fill with more delight than 50 common years could ever contain."

I had Frankie for ten years. It seems like a butterfly life, so short, yet so packed in. He had such a ferocious zest for life.

In the course of ten years, he changed me, he changed lives, he saved lives. We stand on this ground today honestly because of the fireworks Penny Miller saw the moment they locked eyes. He is an energy that demanded you be drawn into him. He demanded love, he demanded adoration, he demanded attention. If I had his capabilities as a woman, I would rule the world.

This dog required all of us to raise him, love him, and serve him.

He leaves a legacy- how many dogs leave a legacy? Usually only a combination of Jesus and a supermodel!

He worked so hard, but here, now, his work is done.....yet I am sure whether we see it now, or in the future, Frankie will still mould us in the way he sees fit."

He was the luckiest dog in the world, and he paved the way for other dogs to be every bit as fortunate as he was. Frankie,

PENNY MILLER

all of the dogs at the cabin were saved because of you and your big, big magic.

So, from Lil Kim, Boris Karloff, Ilsa, Luna shoes, Cody, Aldous Huxley, Murray, Amy, Errol Flynn, Donald O'Connor, Naomi Watts, Reese Witherspoon, Sally Field, Trudy, Ozzy Osbourne, Frannie, Quentin Crisp, Juju, Fiona, Snazzy, Gilda Radner and Patton…

Thankyou Big Boy, and goodnight.